the write words

6,500 phrases, puns, idioms and expressions
to help you write your headlines and copy faster

lizette resendez

the write words

ISBN: 9781703750584

Imprint: Independently published

DEDICATION

*For my parents, Arnoldo and Janie Resendez, who filled every home
we ever had with books, filled my summer weekends
with trips to the library, and filled me with the confidence
that I could do anything I put my mind to.*

the write words

CONTENTS

ACKNOWLEDGMENTS

To my husband, Bret Hirsch – my biggest champion for the last 17 years. No matter what crazy idea I get in my brain, you're 100% behind it. Thank you for tolerating the nights when I had to work on this and left you on the couch to watch Marvel movies on your own (although you probably didn't mind that at all, huh?) And thank you for grabbing our crying son from his bed in the middle of the night to bring him into ours when I was locked in the guestroom working on this. I love you.

To my son Elliott Hirsch, my one and only, who tolerated my typing on my laptop in the middle of countless Houston Astros baseball games and Texas A&M football games. You certainly already have a way with words at just four years old, and I hope you grow up to love writing and reading as much as your parents.

To Katherine Jankovic. I so appreciate your enthusiasm, collaboration and "designer" eyes on this book. You made the process of brainstorming, collaborating and designing a modern and fresh book cover effortless and fun. I can't wait for our next project together.

To Chad White, for your guidance and encouragement when I first pitched this book idea to you back in December 2018. I could not have done this without the insights you gathered and shared from publishing your own book, *Email Marketing Rules*. Your advice made the process so much easier. Good luck on your next one!

And to Sarah Ostiz. I'm so glad I stumbled across your profile on my frantic search for a Microsoft Word formatting expert. I could not have taken these pages to the finish line without your mad formatting skills, and I'm so grateful to you.

INTRODUCTION

True story: I didn't know what a copywriter was when I applied for my first copywriting job at Williams-Sonoma in 2005. That is, until someone reminded me that the *Seinfeld* character, Elaine Benes, was a copywriter for the J. Peterman catalog. All I knew, thanks to the job posting, was that the job required lots of writing. And being a recent graduate with a journalism degree and internships at magazines and newspapers under my belt, I knew I could write. So I went to the interview, smiled a lot, pretended I knew exactly what a copywriter did, shared some work samples, passed the copywriting test, and what do you know, I got the job!

My new job would entail writing both descriptive and marketing copy for Pottery Barn Kids and Teen furniture, bedding and accessories across their monthly catalogs, websites and email campaigns.

It was so much fun (and just cool) until I realized after a few weeks that I had to write about the same things over and over and over again. Striped bedding, floral bedding, checkered bedding, Bunk beds, queen beds, trundle beds, floral curtains, floral rugs, floral backpacks, summertime shindigs, back to school study spaces, and holiday gatherings.

There was so much to write, and so little time to come up with something fresh for every asset I was writing for. I was writing and editing copy across catalogs, web, email marketing campaigns, social media and in-store signage. I needed a way to keep track of every idea I had – good and bad – for every item I'd had to write for, so that if I needed those good or bad ideas in the future, I'd have a nice little repository ready to pull from.

Need a headline about the new floral bedding for page 2 of the summer catalog? You got it.

Need a "punny" subject line for that email marketing campaign that goes out tomorrow morning promoting our holiday collections? Done!

No time? No coffee? No problem!

So how was I doing it all?

Well, I had been keeping a stack of at least 15 5x7" lined pages from a spiral notebook at my desk at all times with all of my brainstorm words, phrases and ideas for every topic I'd ever had to write about. It was the only way to keep track of those good (and yes, many bad) ideas so that I could pull from them in a pinch.

And pull from them, I did.

Before I knew it, those lined pieces of paper, which I'd had to re-staple every few months when the corners of the pages became so worn that the staple simply fell out, were becoming so soft, almost see-through, that they were starting to fall apart. And I'd only been at the company for a little over a year!

Worried that the janitor might see this sad, faded stack of hastily stapled papers and think it was trash (I'm telling you, the papers were looking *rough*), I decided it was time to transfer those ideas to the 21st century and into my computer.

So I opened a fresh Microsoft Word document on my computer and started transferring my ideas. I created one Word document per topic. Before I knew it, I had at least 30 different files covering topics like holidays, sports, prints and colors.

And while I left my job at Williams-Sonoma in 2011, I took all of those Word docs I'd built to every job after and kept on adding to them as I moved from one company, industry and product to another.

My copywriting skills have since taken me from San Francisco to New York and back home to Texas. I've written for just about every medium available: newspapers, magazines, websites, email marketing campaigns, catalogs, social media, in-store signage, RFPs, pitch decks and more. And like any seasoned copywriter, I've had to learn and write about a variety of topics and industries, including fashion, software, travel, toys, financial services, automotive, insurance and even cloud technology.

Those Microsoft Word docs have swelled to over 130 topics and subcategories. (I wish I could say I still have that original stack of 5x7" pages, but they were just not tough enough to survive my Marie Kondo-inspired purge of 2016.)

Now, 15 years after that first copywriting job at Williams-Sonoma, I figured it was time to make it official and transfer these ideas and Microsoft Word docs to another format – an actual book.

I hope this book will help those fellow and future copywriters during their writer's block moments when they just don't know what else to say about that darn polka dot rug they've had to write about for three seasons in a row. Or that new small business owner come up with fun copy for their own website or promotions. Or that blogger who thinks the headline for his or her next blog post could and should be a little punchier.

My hope is that this book becomes as well worn, dog-eared and soft as that stack of 5x7" lined pages I had at my desk as a 20-something copywriter who was just learning what it was that a copywriter actually does. Enjoy!

HOW TO USE THIS BOOK

This is not the type of book I ever thought I'd write. You know, the next Great American Novel. A book where you start at the beginning and end at the end – although you can totally do that with this one if you feel so inclined. With this book, you can just flip through to see if anything inspires you, or check out the table of contents to get an idea of the types of topics I've included here.

Need to write something right now? See if the topic or category you're writing about is in here and flip to that page. Scroll through some of the words and phrases I have for that topic or category and see if any of them fits or gets your wheels turning.

Some lists are definitely longer than others simply because I wrote about some topics more frequently. And if you need additional inspiration, check out a few quick copywriting tips I've gathered on the next page or some of my favorite resources at the back of this book.

A FEW QUICK COPYWRITING TIPS

Books upon books have been written about how to be a great copywriter. So I won't waste your time diving too deep into the process. But I *would* like to share a few tips I've picked up along the way that can help make writing copy and headlines a little easier and more impactful.

Ask Questions

Of course, you should always start with the who, what, where, when, why, and how, but you should also always ask, "So what?" That's probably the most important question. Your copy should answer that to ultimately help readers decide why your business or product or service is exactly what they need.

"So, before you begin the writing, be sure you know the purpose or mission or objective of every piece of content that you write. What are you trying to achieve? What information, exactly, are you trying to communicate? And why should your audience care?"

– Ann Handley, author of *Everybody Writes*

Know Your Audience

I'll never forget the time I had to write about nightstands for children's bedrooms during my first job as a copywriter for Pottery Barn Kids. As a 23-year old, I had absolutely no idea why children would need nightstands by their bed. Seeing my struggle, my manager and editor at the time, Darrah MacLean, told me something to the effect of, "This is not for kids. This is for moms. Moms need somewhere to place all those bedtime books before they turn off the lights." I immediately felt my heart flutter as I imagined my own parents telling me goodnight as a child, and I realized that I wasn't really thinking about my real audience – the parents (duh!).

Think about not only what your audience needs to know, but also what they want to know. What are their struggles? Their concerns? Their fears? Their desires?

What do you want them to think, feel and do once they read your copy? Outlining that will help you write copy that really speaks to them.

Know Your Medium

Direct marketing copy is different from editorial copy. For instance, longer copy is fine in a magazine editorial piece or a blog post, but in an email marketing campaign, where you have less than a second to get a subscriber's attention, your headline and copy need to work a lot harder and faster. Your copy should fit the purpose of the medium you're writing for.

"Get rid of half the words on each page,
then get rid of half of what's left."

– Steve Krug, author of *Don't Make Me Think*

Have Fun with Your Words (and Online Resources)

Depending on the brand and audience you're writing for, you can really have some fun with words, phrases and headlines. But it definitely takes a little more creativity. If you're not as creative or "punny" as you'd like to be, here's what a typical process might look like when I'm trying to come up with something clever.

So, let's say you're writing about stripes.

1.   If you don't want to actually use the word "stripes", then just go somewhere like www.thesaurus.com to find an alternate. There you'll find

words like ribbon, streak, band, etc. Pick the one that works best for your brand and product.

2.   Now maybe you work for a very playful brand, like J.Crew or Poketo, that's more open to fun puns and wordplay in their headlines and copy. Try searching for idioms and similar phrases online at sites like www.idioms.thefreedictionary.com. In the search box, type "stripe" and see what you get.

3.   You might get something like "Change one's stripes" or "Show your stripes", both of which could be perfect for a fashion magazine spread.

4.   However, maybe you don't want to use the word "stripes" because, oh I don't know, the VP at the company hates that word. So try to search for idioms with the word "band" or "streak" and you might get something like "Winning streak" or "Strike up the band."

5.   If you still haven't found just the right phrase, you can go to www.rhymezone.com and see what other words rhyme with "stripes" that might open the door to additional headline ideas. Words that rhyme with stripes could include pipe, ripe or swipe.

So how about changing "Swipe right", which is slang for really liking something, to "Stripe right"? Can you see how a fun headline like that could also influence the design of a layout?

6.   Now search for idioms using those rhymed words to see if you can produce any other fun options by just replacing the rhymed word with "stripe". For instance, the idiom "pipe dream" can become "stripe dream". And "ripe for the picking" could turn into "stripes for the picking". Cute, right?

7.   Still drawing a blank? Try doing a topic search on scrapbooking sites, for instance www.scrapbook.com, for more inspiration.

8.   Now, all those semi-good ideas you gathered during your online search? Add them to your own brainstorming documents (or pencil them into this book!) in case you think you can use them in the future.

9.   Share your clever new headline ideas with the designer or marketing team and bask in all the glory and praise.

"Make it simple. Make it memorable.
Make it inviting to look at. Make it fun to read."

– Leo Burnett

For more inspiration, check out **Additional Resources** on pg. 213. Now let's dig into some fun words and phrases I've gathered along the way. I hope they inspire you and help you write copy that's all your own.

SECTION 1:

COLORS AND PRINTS

CAMO

Blend in

Blend the rules

Bring the outside inside

Call of the wild

Camo blend in

Camo connection

Camo that stands out

Camouflage

Can't-miss camo

Cover girl

Cover up with camo

Cover your back with camo

Cover your bases with camo

Cover your tracks

Get cozy with camo

Go undercover with camo

Go wild

Hide out

Hideaway

Into the wild

On the hunt for camo?

Show your camo

Spot your sleep space some camo

Stand out

Take cover

Take cover with camo

Undercover

Walk on the wild side

Wild about camo

Wild card

Wild for camo

Wildest dream

COLORS

BLACK

Black attack

Back in black

Black is back

Black list

Black magic

Black on track

Bold blacks

Bold in black

Clean slate

In the black

Ink

Lead the pack in black

Onyx

Pitch black

Slated for…

That's so raven

Think ink

BLACK & WHITE

B&W

Black & white affair

Black & white effects

Black & white hot nights

Black & white is gold

Black & white moves

Black & white night

Black on white

Black-and-white out

Black, meet white.

Black, white & now!

Black, white & wow

Bold and bright black and white

Bold black pops on bright white

Dream in black & white

Go mono in black & white

Graphic black & white

High contrast

Instant impact

Life in black & white

Love in black & white

Make it black & white

Mod

Opposites attract

Perfect contrast

Retro

See the world in black & white

Two-tone pair

Zebra

BLUE

Baby blues

Blue blood

Blue cues

Blue crush

Blue fly

Blue moon

Blue notes

Blue state

Blue streak

Blue's clues

Bolt from the blue

Cerulean

Cobalt

Cue the blue

Do the blue

Indigo

In the blue

In the navy

Mad about blue

Once in a blue moon

Out of the blue

Sapphire gimlet

Shades of blue

True blues

Varsity blues

Witches' blue

GOLD

Gilded age

Gilt-y pleasures

Gleaming metallics

Go for the gold

Gold standard

Golden opportunity

Good as gold

Heart of gold

Metallic in the mix

Metals in the mix

Must-have metallic

Solid gold

GRAY

Go gray

Going gray

Gorgeous grays

Gray area

Gray matter(s)

Gray play

Gray streak

Gray way

Gray zone

Play with gray

Quicksilver

Shades of gray

Silver lining

Smoky

GREEN

A need for green

Change of greenery

Dream in green

Eat your greens

Emerald city

Emerald glow

Enjoy the greenery

Go for green

Go green

Green acres

Green dreams

Green energy

Green galore

Green mean

Green means go

Green party

Green spree

Green streak

Green with envy

Green's the thing.

Greener pastures

It's a green thing.

Jaded

Keen green

Keen on green?

Leafy green

Leaves of grass

O.M.Green.

Olive branch

On a green spree

Think green

ORANGE

Atomic orange

Orange blossom

Orange county

Orange crush

Orange juice

Orange peel

Orange sky

Orange zest

Tangerine dream

Tangerine zing

PINK

At first blush

Berry bomb

Berry buzz

Berry crush

Berry pretty

Berry splash

Cotton-candy

Make me blush

Pass the pastels

Pastel crush

Pastels, please

Perfect pastels

Pink punch

Pinky swear

Pretty in pink

Pretty pinks

Pretty plumage

Think pink

Tickled pink

Ultra pink

Watermelon

PURPLE

Grape expectations

Grapevines

Graphic violets

Lavender

Luxe lavender

Punchy purples

Pure purple

Purple power

Ultraviolet

Vivid violets

RED

Cardinal

Code red

Crimson tide

In the red

Red alert

Red army

Red hot

Red state

Rose-colored glass

Scarlet fever

Seeing red

The red party

WHITE

Alabaster brights

Bright whites

Do the white thing

Great whites

In the white

In the white spot

Ivory tower

On the white track

Pearl drops

Pearl snaps

Pearls of wisdom

Pearly brights

Pearly greats

Pearly mates

Pearly whites

Set things white

The white stuff

White magic

White noise

White now

White on!

White side up

White to work

YELLOW

Bee a friend

Catch the sun

Lemon

Lemony fresh

Like the sun

Liquid sunshine

Mellow in yellow

Moment in the sun

Place in the sun

Sun worshipper

Sunny shade

Sunshine state

Yellow brick road

Yellow flutter

Yield to yellow

COLORS

All that glitters

All-out bold colors

Believe in color

Bright delights

Bright hot

Bright stuff

Bright touch

Bring on neon

Call to color!

Call to the colors

Candy swirls

Change color

Color adaptation

Color balance

Color beat

Color blindness

Color by numbers

Color chart

Color code

Color combos

Color connection

Color cool

Color correct

Color crush

Color cube

Color field

Color guard

Color in motion

Color is key

Color lines

Color match

Color matters

Color mix

Color notes

Color play

Color reaction

Color refresh

Color rocks!

Color sense

Color smart

Color theory

Color vision

Color wonder

Color your world

Cool color

Crazy brights

Crazy cool color

Dream in color

Eye-catching

Eye-popping

Fall for color

Field of color at your feet

Find your color

Fluorescent

Flying colors

Full spectrum

Get color smart

Heavy metal

Hi-Fi

High-contrast color

Hot brights

Hues

Light & color

Living in color

Local color

Made in the shade

Made in your shade

Mix it up

Neon bomb

Neon dream

Neon nights

Neon now

Neutrals and naturals

New hue, new you

Paint by numbers

Palette

Pass the pastels

Pastel crush

Pastels, please

Pattern detection

Perfect pastels

Play with color

Radiant

Rainbow bright

Rainbow glow

School of color

Shades of fall

Shades of light

Show your colors

Spot your space some color

Spring forward with color

Spring color rollout

Spring is all about color

Sprinkle color everywhere

Sprinkle splashes of color

Turn up the volume

Versatile color

What's your color?

Which hue are you?

Which hue is YOU?

FLORALS

Awesome blossoms

Bedecked in blooms

Belle fleur

Best buds

Bloomin' marvelous

Blossom

Blossom forth

Bring into bloom

Come into bloom

Cream of the crop

Crop

Crop up

Daisy daze

Far-out florals

Field day

Field of color

Floral fixation

Flower girl

Flower power

Frame of flowers

Fresh batch of blossoms

Fresh crop

Full bloom

Garden bed

Garden fresh

Garden gems

Garden grove

Garden of delights

Garden party

Garden sweet/suite

Garden variety

Garden view

Have a field day

How does your garden grow?

In bloom

In blossom

In full bloom

Lead the field

Mad mix of florals

Mixed bouquet

Moody blooms

Petal-perfect picks

Pick some flowers this season

Plant the seed

Plucky charm

Poppy love

Power of flowers

Room to bloom

Rosy outlook

Spring greens

Stem to stem

*For more inspiration, see
Gardening on pg 88.

PLAID

Breaking plaid

Check it!

Check it out

Check mix

Check mate!

Check off your list

Check up

Check, please

Clad in plaid

Double-check

Grid lock

Grid marks

Mad about plaid

Mad for plaid

Off the grid

Pattern

Pattern behavior

Pattern check

Pattern detection

Plaid clad

Plaid fad

Plaid hatter

Plaid rags

Plaid tidings

Rad plaid

Rain check

Reality check

Spot check

Tartan

Triple check

RINGS, CIRCLES, DOTS

Ace in the hole

Bright spot of your day

Come full circle

Connect the dots

Go full circle

Go/jump through hoops

Hit the spot

Hole

Hole in one

Hole up next to

Hole-y mole-y

Holes

Hoop dreams

Hot spot

I spy with my eye

In the loop

Must-see-through

On the dot

On the spot dots

Put a ring on it

Ring in the new

Ring out the old

Rings

Run rings around

Score a hole in one with

See-through circles

Seeing spots

Soft spot

Spot-on Style

Sweet spot

Through the hoop

We've made a hole in

You've spotted

SECTION 2:

ENTERTAINMENT, MUSIC AND MOVIES

MAGIC

A whole new world

Aim for the stars

Aladdin

Be our guest

Believe

Bewitching

Bibbidi bobbidi boo

Bring magic to the…

Bringing magic

Bringing magic to life

Bringing magic to the …

Circle of life

Creating magic together

Do the impossible

Dream big

Dreams are made of…

Enchanting

Even miracles take a little time

Fairies

Happily ever after

Hocus pocus

How far I'll go

It's a small world after all

It's off to work we go

Magic kingdom

Magic stone

Magic sword

Magic touch

Magic wand

Magical

Make impossible possible

Mysterious

Never never land

Once upon a dream

Open sesame

Part of your world

Pixie dust

Prince Charming

Scepter

Secret

Secret to our success

Shazam

Shoot for the stars

Sorcerer

Spellbinding

Spellbound

Stars aligning

Supercalifragilistic-
expialidocious

The bare necessities

The happiest place on Earth

The wonderful world of
Disney

Trance

Where magic happens

Wish upon a star

Wizardry

Work our own magic

Works like magic

World of magic

World of miracle and magic

You can fly

MOVIE WORDS, SAYINGS AND QUOTES

2 thumbs up

3D

A "reel" movie set

A *reel* set for movie marathons

A-list

And action!

And cut!

And scene!

Awards night

Blockbuster

Bloopers

Body double

Box office

Break a leg

Buzz

Cameo

Camera

Casting couch

Chick flick

Cinema

Cinematic

Cinephile

Cliffhanger

Clip from a movie

Comic relief

Concession stand

Cue cards

Director's chair

Director's cut

Double feature

Encore!

Favorite flick

Feature film

Feature presentation

Film

Film clip

Film fest

Final cut

Flash forward

Found footage

Four stars

Freeze frame

Indie films

In the limelight

Lead role

Lights, camera, action

Magic hour

Movie buff

Movie marathons

Movie night

Movie night makeover

Movie night must-haves

Movie night party

Movie reel

Movie-goer

Moviephile

Netflix

Popcorn

Premiere

Rated E for everyone

Rating

Red carpet

Reel

Remake

Rising star

Roll the credits

Rough cut

Scene-stealer

Set the scene

Setting the scene

Star-studded cast

Supporting role

Take one

The show must go on

Thumbs up

Ticket holder

Ticket stub

Triple threat

VIP

Work the camera

TECH

MUSIC AND TECH

Be kind. Rewind.

Be cool. Sync up.

Big hits for music fans

Break records

Change your tune

Do you hear what I hear?

Face the music

Get in sync

Get in tune

Get pumped

Hook up

In tune

It's on!

Keep it all in sync

Mix it up

Mix master

On our playlist

Out of tune

Play DJ

Play it cool

Play it smart!

Playlist

Playlist. Work list. … list.

Plug in

Plug in & play

Plug In. Play. Kick back.

Recharge.

Plug in. Play. Recharge.

Plug in, rock out

Power play

Pump it up

Ready to rock?

Ready, set, rock!

Rock 'n' roll model

Rock on…

Rock your tunes

Shuffle

Stay with the shuffle

Stop the music

Sweet hookup

Sync up

Sync or Shuffle

Tune in to more …

Tech mix

Tech time

Tech, please!

This rocks

Total volume control

Tune in to …

Tune up

Turn it up

Turn up the music

Turn up your tunes

Volume control

Wake up call!

What's your jam?

SMARTPHONES

10-4

A case for …

A case of …

Airplane mode

Answer the call

Call me

Call me, maybe

Call up…

Calling all …

Close calls

Did you get my message?

Do not disturb

Exchange numbers

Give me a ring

Goodbye

Hang up

Hello, it's me….

I just called …

In sync with …

It's for you…

Last call!

Leave a message

Make the call

No, you hang up

Phone zone

Ring, ring…

Screen time

Swipe left

Swipe right

Text me

Tough call

Wake-up call

What's your call sign?

What's your number?

You called?

APPS

An app-y event

An app-y medium

App it up

App out

App-shy

App-tastic

App-titude

Apps are where it's at

Apps on tap

Apps to the max

App-y camper

Appy-y go lucky

App-y hour

C'mon, get app-y

Couldn't be app-ier

Do the max with apps

Do your app-y dance

Got apps?

Got these apps?

Must-have apps

Sn-app to it!

Snap up these apps

Tried these apps?

SECTION 3:

FASHION AND RETAIL

BEST SELLERS

[brand] [customer] fave

[brand] [customer] heart...

[brand] [customer] pick!

[brand] [customers] love...

[year] favorites

All our greatest for [year]

All the hits

Arrivals

Biggest hits of [year]

Crowd pleasers

Customer favorites

Discover our top picks

Essential picks

Essentials

Everyone's crazy for 'em!

Favorites

Flying off the rack...

Get the goods!

Greatest hits

Have to have!

Hip picks

Hits

Insider favorites

Key essentials

Looks

Love, need, have to have!

Most coveted styles

Most popular pick!

Must-haves

Necessary style

Off the charts: shop the greatest hits of [year]

On every [customer's] list

On the [brand] hit list...

Over 200 new ...

Pick your favorites

Picks

Required styles

Shop these popular picks!

Spring style must-haves

The essentials

The greatest of [year]

The latest must-haves

The most in-demand items

Top customer favorites

Top essentials

Top items in demand

Top picks

Top trends

Top xx hits of [year]

Ultimate top picks

Updates

Voted most popular

Want the goods?

FASHION, IN PIECES

ACCESSORIES

A fine finish

A jewelry affair.

Accessories make the girl.

Accessories make the outfit

Adorn

All in the details

All the small things

Arm candy

Big and bold

Big bets

Bold baubles

Bold moves

Bright

Bright on trend

Complete your look

Crowning touch

Decorative arts

Delicate matters

Divine details

Divine details. Master pieces.

Embellishments

Extra, extra…

Find your finish

Fine finish

Finishing touch

Fun, love & jewelry for all.

Get it on.

Gleam & glimmer

Go for the glow.

Grand finale

In the details

Intricate

It's a jewelry life.

It's all about the extras

It's in the details.

It's the little things…

Last act

Last steps

Left, bright and center

Let's hook you up.

Little extras

Little luxuries

Look on the bright side.

Love at first sight.

Love. Life. Jewelry.

Luxe be a lady.

Master pieces

On the bright track

Opulent

Pieces

Serves you bright

Shimmer & shine

Sparkling contrast

That's a wrap

The extras

The final flourish

The final touch

The finishing touch

The finishing touch starts here.

The luxe life.

Top off your look

Trimmings

We love jewelry.

We're obsessed.

Wrap up

BRAS

Barely there

Bounce-free

Bra-mance

Bra-some

Get hooked

Get the hook up

Holds 'em in

Hooked on a feeling

Keeps 'em in place

Left hook

Let's hook you up

More control

More hold

No bounce

No-move

Ready to get hooked up?

Rein in

Right hook

Shock absorbent

Shock-free

Solid hold

Stay-put shape

You'll be hooked…

COATS/JACKETS

A case for coats

All wrapped up

Chic

Chic Cover-ups

Coat check

Coat tails

Coat tales

Coats of note

Coverups

Don't leave without your coat/bag/scarf

Fresh coat of polish

Grab your coat

Hide

Jacket magic

Jacket required

Just jackets

Peacoats, puffers, parkas

Rock the coat

Rock the jacket

Smoking jacket

Straight jacket

That's a wrap

THE jacket

Under wraps

Wrap it up

DENIM

A denim do: brights!

Denim does it

Denim done bright!

Dressed up denim

Dressed up in denim

It's a denim day

Jeanius

Jeans

Jeans addiction

Our don't-miss denim

DRESSES

A dress request

All dressed up

Best dressed

Change of a dress

Dress behavior

Dress bets

Dress code

Dress is more!

Dress obsessed

Dress quest

Dress the part

Dress to impress

Dress up

Dress you up in my love

Dressed for success

Dressed to kill

Dressed to the nines

Dressing

Forms of a dress

From 9 to 5

Girl's dress friend

It's all about the dress

Morning meeting to happy hour

Play dress up

Power dressing

Quest for the dress

Ready, set, dress!

Strict dress code

Summer frocks to rock!

The beautiful, versatile dress

The best of dresses

The best of the dresses

Ultimate multitasker

Wear-everywhere dress

Work, weekend and everything in between

Workweek to weekend

LACE

A case of lace

Ace of lace

All about lace…

All over lace

Amazing lace

Embrace the lace

Got a case of lace

Gotta love lace!

Lace alert

Lace cadet

Lace is it

Lace out

Lace up!

Lace yourself

Lace-scapade

Lacy layers (we're obsessed!)

Let's lace it!

Lotsa lace

Love me some lace!

Ooh la lace

Our lace is tops!

Our latest obsession: lace!

The case for lace

The lace is on!

We can't get enough lace

We heart these lacy layers

We l-o-v-e l-a-c-e

LAYERS

Layer by layer

Layer down

Layer lowdown

Layer player

Layer up

Lowdown on layers

Play with layers

MESH/SHEER TRENDS

Fresh with mesh

Get mesh

Get mesh with me

In the mesh

Lighten up

Mesh

Mesh code

Mesh effects

Mesh fest

Mesh is more

Mesh it out

Mesh madness

Mesh mix

Mesh refresh

Mesh start

Mesh to the max

Mesh together

Mesh up

Mesh with you

Must-get mesh

Obsessed with mesh

Press the mesh

Refreshed our mesh

Sheer bliss

Sheer delight

Sheer force

Sheer genius

Sheer heaven

Sheer joy

Sheer love

Sheer madness

Sheer magic

Sheer perfect

Sheer up

NAIL/LIP

A little polish

Best mani ever

Buff them

Chip…

Click / tap

Coat of polish

Coats of notes

Cut cuticles…

Lacquer

Nail art

Nail dotters

Nail file

Nail it

Nail your look

Nailed it!

No bumps, chips or smudges

On the nail

Polished to perfection

Pro painter

PANTIES/UNDERGARMENTS

Bottoms up!

Code: Panty!

Code: Undies

Panty bash

Panty blast!

Panty break!

Panty craze!

Panty crush

Panty fest

Panty fever!

Panty fiesta

Panty fight

Panty madness

Panty obsess fest!

Panty overload

Panty pileup!

Panty play

Panty rally

Panty rave

Panty rush

Panty score!

Panty up!

Panty-ganza

Panty-mania

Panty-rama!

PANTS

Best bottoms

Bottoms up

Brilliant bottoms

Brilliant pants

By the seat of your pants

Charm the pants off

Do the legwork

Fancy pants

Get to the bottom of things

Hotstepper

Kick in the butt

Kick it up a notch

Kick things up!

Kickin' things up

Our top bottoms

Race to the bottom

Rock bottom

Seat of your pants

Smarty pants

Step up your style

Walk on the wild side

Wear the pants

RUFFLES

A light border of ruffles

A little ruffle goes a long way...

All ruffled up

Bands of ruffles

Blooming ruffles

Craving a little flounce?

Crinkled

Feathered

Feathery

Flirty

Flowing ruffles

Folded ruffles

For the frill of it

Frilly

Fun & flirty flounce

Gathered ruffles

Generous row of ruffles

Ivory ruffles

Just for frills!

Lavish ruffles

Let's flounce!

Little flounce, big splash

Mini ruffles

Oversized ruffles

Raging ruffles

Rings of ruffles

Romantic ruffles

Rows of ruffles

Ruffly ruffles

So flouncy, so flirty

Soft

Structured ruffles

Swirls of ruffles

Translucent ruffles

Understated ruffles

SHORTS

A shoutout to shorts season!

A shoutout to shorts!

Get shortie

Get shorty…

Hey short stuff!

Life's too short

Short change

Short circuit

Short end

Short run

Short shorts

Short stop

Short story

Shorty shoutout

Shorts sighted!

STRIPES

Between the lines

Fall in line

Fine line

Fine lines

Party lines

Show your stripes

Stand out in stripes

Straight edge

Stripe a pose

Stripe hype

Stripe it up!

Stripe the right note

Toe the line

Walk the line

Walk the lines

White stripes

SUITS

Follow suit

Head to toe

Look sharp

Mix, match and make them
your own

One suit fits all

One suits all

Perfectly suited

Polished

Sharp

Sharp suiter

Sharp suiting

Sharp suits

Suit up!

Suit yourself

Suited for success

Suited in style

Suited to a T

Suited up

Uniquely suited

Well-suited

Your strong suit

SWEATERS

Best sweaters for spring
weather

Better sweater

Big-time chill chasers.

Buh-bye chilly days.

Bundle up!

Bundle up! It's sweater
weather...

Chase the chill with cozy
sweaters

Cold comforts

Cold holder

Cold shoulder

Cold weather meets its match

Control the cold

Cozy sweaters for
winter weather!

Cozy, casual, chic

Extra warm for extra
chilly days

Get knit

Heavier weight to chase
the chill

Hold back the cold

It's cold out there!

Kill the chill

Knit hits

Knit parade

Knit picks

Layers we love

Luxe fall layers

Luxe layers

Made to chase the chill.

Ready, set, sweaters!

Take your (knit) pick

Ward off winter weather

SWIMSUITS

Beauty & the beach

Bikini crossing

Cute suits

Fun and flirty

Hit the sand

In the swim of things

Just add water

Life's a beach!

Make a splash

Strong suit

Suit pursuit

Suit up

Suit yourself

Super cute suits

Sweet suit

Swim fan

The scene, the style, the suits!

Tie one on

What suit's you?

TOPS/TEES/BLOUSES

Come out on top

Cross your tees

Fall for our tops

From top to bottom

Get to the top

Hard to top…

It's tee time

Layer on the tops

Layering to a tee

Over the top

Race to the top

Start at the top

Take it from the top

Tee up!

Textured tops

This sale is tops

Top flight

Top gun

Top it off

Top news

Top notch

Top off

Top off the season

Top savings for fall

Top secret

Top service

Top story

Top that

Top to toe

Top-notch savings

Topography

Tops for fall, tops for all!

FASHION TRENDS AND STYLES

All-out brights	Cool rider
All-out color	Country cozy
Best in fest	Downtown…
Blue blood	Eclectic
Bohemian beauty	Everyday glamour
Bohemian bounty	Fashion face-off
California cool	Fashion forward
Cavalry calling	Fest forever
Chain gang	Festival best
Chalet chic	Festival bound
Checks mix	Festival fashion
Cirque du chic	Festival faves
Citrus burst	Festival ready
City chic	Flash of brilliance
City girl	Fresh
Clash mob	Full spectrum
Coastal prep	Glam squad
Concert cutie	Gleam & glimmer
Cool and classic	Gothic glamour
Cool for Coachella	Graphic conditions

Graphic content

Graphic edge

Graphic glamour

Graphic jam!

Graphic report

Graphic update

Graphic zone

Haute couture

Head trip

Heavy metal

Heirloom jewels

It's eclectic

Kick it

Lavish print

Layers

Love fest

Lush be a lady

Lush textures

Lust list

Luxe touch

Make a statement

Make the varsity letter grade

Master pieces

Max

Megawatt jeans

Metal shop

Moto to the max

Music festival fashion

Must-get

Must-have

Nautical chic!

Needles and pins

On the edge

Pattern behavior

Pattern boldness

Pattern detection

Pep squad (peplum)

Pop of color

Pretty preppy

Print remix

Prints charming

Punk moment

Ready to rock

Rebel yell (turn up
the volume)

Rock

Rock 'n' roll model

Shimmer & shine

Signature style

Simply relaxed

Sporty

Sporty silhouettes

Spot-on

Spunk

Star style

Street chic

Street smarts

Street style

Strike gold

Studded, pierced, zippered,
shot through with metal

Style

Summer chic

Swim fan

The edge on leggings

Tough gal

Tough love

Tough stuff

Track stars (take a
victory lap…)

Uptown chic

Urban jungle

Velvet goldmine

Visual arts

Winter chic

Word on the street

Works of art

SHOES

A step ahead

Boot camp

Do flips

Do the legwork

Every step you take

Fast feet

Flip out

Flip your lid

Flippin' amazing

Foot in the door

Foot traffic

From tip to toe

Get in line…

Get the boot

Head to toe

Heart over heels

Heel

High

Hike

Hit the sale

Hit your stride

Hoof it

Hot heels

Hot on the heels!

In step

Kick it

Leg up

Leg-lengthening

March

Mind your step

Need a lift?

On the flipside

On your toes

One step ahead

Out of step

Pace

Platform pumps

Race

Reboot

Roundin' up our flip flops

Shoe shine

Sole mate

Stand tall

Start on the right foot

Stay on your toes

Step aside

Step by step

Step in the right direction

Step it up

Step on it

Step right up

Step up

Stepped up style

Stride

Tip to toe

Toe the line

Toe the mark

Toes

Traffic

Travel

Tread

Trek

Walk

Walk right up

Walk talk

Watch your steps

Well-heeled

BOOTS/BOOTIES

Astute boots

Boot pursuit

Boot up

Boots mean business

Commute boots

Cute boots

Re-boot for winter

Salute to boots

The boot route

We salute boots

Winter re-boot

EVENING

A little glitter goes a long way

All that glitters

Brilliant

Fancy feet

Fancy footwork

Glisten

Glitz

Shine

Sparkle

Splendid

Spotlight

Twinkle

Twinkle toes

FLATS

Fab flats

Fabulous flats

Fall for flats

Flat out perfect

Flats season

Flats to fall for

Flawless flats

Love those flats!

On the level

The low down on flats

Twinkle toes

HEELS

All the heels

At your heels

Bring to a heel

Call to heels

Dig heels in

Drag your heels

From head to heels

Haute heels

Head over heels

Kick your heels up

King of the heel

Leg-lengthening dream

Sexy stiletto or sensible block heel?

Swoon for a stiletto

Take to the heels

Well-heeled

WEDGES

Dizzying heights

High and mighty

High time

Higher ground

In high demand

Living on the wedge

Need a lift?

On a high note

On the edge

Sky high

Swoon-worthy wedges

The height of...

SECTION 4:

FOOD AND DRINK

CANDY

...to crave

Air-light...

Airy

Barely there

Bonbon

Candy hearts

Candy shop

Cotton candy-light

Crave

Crave new...

Craving...

Dainty

Dolce vita

Eye candy

Fluff

Frosting

Get a sugar high

Get your fix.

Guilt-free

In a rainbow of colors

Jam

Light as cotton candy

Lightweight

Little sweet things

New crave-worthy...

Our sweetest ... yet

Powder puff

Pretty sweet

Rainbow brights!

Rainbow of colors

Small wonders

Sugar fix

Sugar high

Sugar rush

Sugar-free

Sugar-sweet

Sweet

Sweet 'n' light

Sweet and light like

Sweet dreams

Sweet little nothings…

Sweet new … to crave

Sweet peek

Sweet peek, unexpectedly
sweet

Sweet talk

Sweet tooth

Sweet treat!

The sweet life

Tooth ache

Ultralight

Unexpectedly sweet

We heart

We're sweet on these
new styles

DRINKS

DRINK	WINE
Another round	A second glass
Big gulp	A spring to savor
Cheers	A taste of spring
Coffee break	Aged
Custom cocktails	Barrel-aged
Drink up	Barrel tasting
Eat, drink, and be merry	Berries
Hydrate	Berry
I'll drink to that	Burgundy
Pour it on	Cellar
Pours	Crush
Sample a sip	Drip
Savory sips	Grape expectations
Sip on this	Grapevine
Take a sip	La vina
Tall drink of…	Merlot
Toast	Oak
We'll drink to that	Passion for life
	Passion for wine

Raise a glass

Raise a toast

Rioja

Savor

Sip

Sparkling sips

Spring escape

Swirl

Swirl, sip, repeat

Taste of the good life

Tasting room

Toast

Vine

Vineyard

Wine time

FOOD

A new spin

A new take

A new twist

All-star combo

Apps

Bake. Decorate. Share!

Bake. Serve. Done!

Beverages

Bite-size

Bites

Bon appetit

Breakfast of champions

Breakfast to go

Brunch

Brunch bunch

Chew it over

Chew on this

Childhood favorite

Comfort food

Crave

Cravings

Crunchy cravings

Cuisine

Culinary

Deck the table

Delectable

Delicacy

Delight

Devour

Dine

Dine in

Dinner for XX

Dinner party

Dinner's on me/us

Dip-and-eat treat

Dish of the day

Easy entrees

Eat out

Exquisite

Fabulous fish

Farm to table	Impress your guests
Feast	In for a treat
Feast your eyes	Individual-sized…
Fire up the grill	Instagram-worthy
Flash frozen	Leftovers
Flavor of the month	Light fare
Flavorful	Lunch bosses
Fruits & veggies	Lunch boxes
Goodie	Meal plans
Goodness	Meal prep
Gourmands and foodies	Must-try dishes
Gourmet	Nibbles
Graze	Party-perfect
Great for grilling	Perfectly ripe
Grill out	Power lunch
Grown-up treat/take	Ready to eat
Have your cake	Ripe for the picking
Healthy, tasty, perfect	Savory
Hearty dishes	Savory snacks
Heavenly	Say cheese
Homemade-style	Serve up…

Sides

Single-serving

Single-shot

Smothered in…

Snacks

Snacks & apps

Spice of life

Spice up

Spicy

Spoon up…

Summer cookout

Sunday morning brunch

Sustainable

Take a bite out of

Takeout

Tangy and sweet

Tasty

Test kitchen

Treat yourself

Treats

Turn on the oven

Wake-up call (breakfast)

What's for breakfast/dinner?

Wine and dine

Wow them

Yummy

Zesty

SECTION 5:

HOLIDAYS AND SPECIAL OCCASIONS

HOLIDAYS / CHRISTMAS

'Tis the season for merry wishes

'Tis the season!

12 days of cheer

12 days of …

A merry & bright sign to shine

All aglow!

All I want for Christmas…

All that glitters

All wrapped up

Be merry & bright!

Better not pout

Check off your gift list!

Check off your list…

Check off your wish list

Chimney

Complete your wish list!

Connected in style

Cool picks for the holidays

Countdown to Christmas!

Cross off your list!

Deck the halls

Deck the halls (skip the malls)

Deck your walls

Deck your walls, merry and bright!

Do you see what I see??

Dreams, love, merry wishes

Fa, la, la, la, laaaaa

Favorite things

For everyone on your list…

For everyone on your nice list!

Genius gifts

Get going for the holidays

Get in the spirit!

Get out your gift list!

Get out your nice list!

Get ready for the holidays

Get ready to cross off your list…

Get the gifts you wish you got

Get what you really wanted…

Gift guide

Gifts to give, gifts to get

Give great

Glad tidings we bring

Go ahead, gift yourself …

Good friends, great gifts!

Got a list? We've got the gift.

Great friends, great gifts!

Great gifts

Happy holidays to you!

Ho, ho, ho!

Holiday charm

Holly, jolly holiday

Holly, jolly, holiday wishes

Hot picks for the holidays!

In the St. Nick of time

It's all on my list

Let it glow, let it glow,
let it glow

Let your heart be bright!

Let your heart be light

Make the season bright

Make your list. Check it twice.

Making a list? Check it
off now!

Merry & bright!

Merry little wishlist

Merry treats

Merry wishes from me to you

More presents, please

Most-wanted gifts

Must-gives

Nice price

Oh, what fun!

On. My. List!

Our favorite picks,
their top gifts

Perfect gifts. Perfect timing!

Present company

Put it all on your list

Ready, set, gift!

Reindeer

Reindeer games

Rejoice!

Santa Claus

Santa Claus is coming to town!

Santa's bag

Season to sparkle

Season's greetings

Secret Santa gifts

Secret Santa picks

Shine a light on peace

Smart gifts

Snowflakes in the air

So gifted

Something just for you!

Sparkle & shine

Still gifts on your wishlist?

Stocking stuffers

Stocking surprises

Stylish list toppers!

Surprises

That's a wrap!

The big wrap up!

The great wrap up!

There's no time like
the present…

Time to gift yourself!

Time to shine

Time to treat yourself!

Tiny treats

Today is the present…

Treat yourself to
something chic…

Unwrap…

Very merry wishes

Want. Them. All!

Warm winter wishes!

We've got your list checked…

Winter must-haves

Winter wonderland

Wishlist-worthy

Wrap up your wishlist with …

Wrapped in merry wishes

Wrapped in very, merry wishes

Your turn

HOLIDAY SAVINGS

'Tis the season for savings!

Ho, ho, ho! Holiday savings
are here!

Holiday savings

Holly jolly savings

List-topping savings

Merry savings

Nice price

Perfect presents at the
perfect price

Perfect presents, perfect price

Savings dash!

Savings on our list

Savings wrap up

Season's savings

Stocking savings

Top-of-the-list gifts at lower-
than-ever prices

Very merry savings

Winter savings

Wish list savings

Wrap up the savings

Wrap up the season

Wrap up your list with...

COLUMBUS DAY

A boatload of…

A new world of…

A shipload of…

A whole new world

Across the Atlantic

Adventure

Ahoy

All aboard

Arrival

At sea

Bon voyage

Captain…

Cargo…

Changing currents

Columbus Day kickoff

Conquer…

Discover

Discover new worlds

Dock here for…

Embark on a…

Explore

Indigenous People's Day

Navigate

New world…

Nina, Pinta, Santa Maria

No need to sail the ocean blue

Rough waters

Sail along

Sail into

Sail through these…

Sale sail…

Savings to blow you out of the water…

Set sail

Ship

Ship, ship hooray

Shipping out

Smooth sailing

Spirit of adventure

This ship's about to sail

Turning tide

Voyage

Waiting for the tide to turn

Your voyage

HALLOWEEN

A chilling celebration!

A creepy, crawly party

A frightful fiesta!

A howlin' celebration

A howlin' good time

A real treat

After the treats are gone

All kinds of spooky

Ball

Bash

Batty

Beware

Bewitching

Blowout

Boo Crew

Candy corn

Celebration

Chilling

Chills and thrills

Come as you aren't

Costume

Crawly

Creature feature

Creatures of the night

Creep it real

Creeping up…

Creepy

Dare to scare

Dark night

Day of the Dead

Dearly departed

Dia de los Muertos

Do you dare?

Don't scream

Don't move

Drink or treat?

Eek!

Eerie

Feast

Fiesta

Fog

Friday the 13th

Fright

Frightening

Frightful

Frightfully

Full moon

Full moon fiesta!

Ghost

Ghoulish

Ghouls

Goblins

Gruesome ghouls

Hair-raisingly

Halloween Happy Hour

Halloween Haunting Hour

Happy haunting!

Haunted

Haute for Halloween

Hocus pocus

Howl

Howl-o-ween

If you dare

Long after midnight

Monster bash

Monster makeover

Monster mash

Monstrous makeover

Moon

Never fear, …are here!

No spells…

No tricks, just treats

Open if you dare

Party

Party-perfect

Party-perfect costumes

Perfect party potions

Potions

Raise some spirits

Shadows

Scare up

Scariest night of the year

Scary

Scary good

Sit for a spell

Skull

Snatch up

Spell

Spirits

Spooktacular

Spooky party

Spooky shindig?

Terror-ific time

The more, the scarier

Thriller

Thrills, spills and chills

Throw a monster bash

To die for

Transform

Treat yourself

Trick or treat

Web of...

Werewolf

What will you be?

Where the wild things are

Wicked fun

Wicked good

Witching hour

Witchy

Your potion for the
perfect party

JULY 4TH / FLAG DAY / PRESIDENTS' DAY

★Boom!★

4th of July

All-American

America the Beautiful

America the Brave

Americana

Baby you're a firework…

Be free, love…

Beach, BBQ, fireworks, sun

Bing Bang Boom!

Born in the USA

Bursting

Celebrate

Cue the fireworks

Dazzle

Explosive summer sale

Fantastic Fourth

Fire up the grill

Firecracker

Fireworks

Fireworks sale

Flag

Fly the Freedom Flag

Forever free

Freedom

Grand old flag

Happy 4th!

Happy Birthday, America

Hey there, firecracker

Home of the free

Last sparks

Let freedom ring

Let the fireworks begin

Let's celebrate

Light up some fireworks…

Light up some sparks

Living in America

My country 'tis of thee

Oh say can you see

Ooh ahh

Ooh ahh yay!

Party in the USA

Patriotic

Promiseland

Ready for some fireworks

Red, white and blue

Red, white and woohoo!

Red, white and you

Rockin' in the free world

Sea to shining sea

See what all the noise is about

Set off sparks

Show your pride

Spark up some fireworks

Sparks

Sparks will fly

Star-spangled tank

Stars and stripes

Stars and stripes forever

Start the fireworks

Start the weekend with a bang!

Starts with a spark

This land is your land

United States

USA

Waving

We the people

Wear your flag

What a show

Yankee Doodle Dandy

3-2-1

ST. PATRICK'S DAY

♣ Lucky You!

A charming St. Patrick's Day

Best o' luck

Best of luck

Blarney

Blarney blast

Click me, I'm Irish

Clover

Don't get pinched

Feel the pinch

Feelin' green

Feelin' Irish

Feeling lucky

Feeling pinched?

Four-leaf

Get lucky

Get lucky with great deals on…

Go "green"

Go green

Gold

Granting wishes

Green

Irish

It's your lucky day!

Luck of the Irish

Lucky

Lucky charms

Lucky deals

Lucky for you

Lucky leaf

Lucky leprechaun

Lucky number

Lucky number 7

Luck of the Irish

Lucky one

Lucky star

Lucky streak

Lucky you

Magically deal-icious

Plenty o' green to save!

Pot of gold

Rainbow

Save a lot o' green

Save green this
St. Patrick's Day

Savin' o' the green

Saving o' the green

Seeing green

St. Patty's Day

The Irish don't have
all the luck

Under the rainbow

Very superstitious

What luck!

You're in luck!

Your luck's in

Your shamrocks are showing

THANKSGIVING

A cornucopia of…

An American Thanksgiving feast

Cold turkey

Dinner's done

Don't be a turkey

Feast on…

Feast your eyes

First, turkey

Gather together

Get dressed for the turkey

Get ready for turkey

Give thanks

Gobble up

Gobble wobble

Gobble, gobble

Gratitude

Happy harvest

Hold the turkey

Hosting Thanksgiving

Let's talk turkey

More stuffed than the turkey

November to remember

Pack your Thanksgiving bags

Pass the potatoes

Stuffed?

Thankful

Thankful for you

Thanksgiving 101

Thanksgiving made easy

Thanksgiving prep

Thanksgiving wishes

Thanksgiving-ready

The turkey's done

Time to give thanks

Tryptophan trance

Turkey day

Turkey lurkey

Turkey time

Turkey, stuffing and…

Turkey, stuffing, gravy,
potatoes

We are thankful

We're stuffed

While the turkey's cooking…

VALENTINE'S DAY

Addicted to…	Eat your heart out
All heart	Electric love
All you need is…	Feel the crush
Be mine	For the love of…
Bee mine	Forget the flowers…
Blind date	From the heart
Bro-mance	Get your heart set on…
Can't buy me love	Handpicked and heartfelt
Change of heart	Happily ever after
Cloud nine	Happy hearts day
Coupled up	Head over boots
Couples getaway	Head over heels
Couples' retreat	Heart
Crazy for …	Heart skips a beat
Cross my heart	Heart to heart
Crush	heart-to-heart
Crush Valentine's Day	Heaven sent
Cuddle up	How sweet it is…
Cupid-approved	It must be love
Cupid, eat your heart out	Kiss this … goodbye

L-O-V-E

Labor of love

Land a smooch

Let's fix you up

Loads to love

Love affair

Love at first sight

Love bombs

Love is blind

Love is in the air

Love notes

Love to bits

Love to pieces

Love, …

Lovebug

More to love

Party for two

Perfect match

Seeing red

Romantic escape

Say "I love you" with…

Sealed with a…

Share the love

Show your … some love

Smitten

So happy together

Spread more love

Sweep off … feet

Sweet talk

Sweet treats

Swipe right

Swoon-worthy

Tea for two

True love

Twosome

Unforgettable

Up your V-Day game

V-day

We <3…

We belong together

We love [blank]. [blank] love(s) us!

Who needs cupid?

Wild at heart

Wild hearts

With love

XOXO

*For more inspiration, see
Weddings on pg 73.

WEDDINGS

A case of you…

A day to remember

A day to…

A night on the town

A night to remember…

A proposal

Adore

Aisle style

All heart

Amour

An evening to remember

Announcement

At first blush

Bead it!

Bearer

Before and after numbers

Belles of the ball

Best dressed guest

Best friend

Best party ever

Bewitched in the big city

Big day

Big love in the cosmopolitan

Black tie

Bloom

Blushing bride

Bold & the beautiful

Book of love

Bouquet

Bride

Bride-to-be

Bubbly

Cake

Cake walk

Celebrate

Ceremony

Champagne

Champagne toast

Charmed

Cherish

Church

City hall

City love…

City sweethearts

City swoon

Cocktails

Color palette

Congratulations

Cosmopolitan couple

Cosmopolitan crush

Cosmopolitan devotion

Cosmopolitan-chic love

Coupled up

Cupid hits the city

Delicate matters

Destination

Devotion

Dream come true

Dream day

Dress-shopping

Engagement

Eternal

Ever after

Every important event in between…

Fairytale

Fall in love with…

Feeling

Fete

First dance

First look

First sight

Flowers

Gallery of gowns

Get married in the city…

Glowing

Go to town

Gorgeous gowns

Gown

Grand entrance

Guest list

Guests

Handle with care

Happily ever after

Happily ever after-party

Happy tears

Happy tiers

Head over heels

Heart

Heart-to-heart

His & hers

Hit the town

Honeymoon

I do

Icing

In love with lace

Inspired

Into the night

Invitation

Invited

Jewels

Joined together

Keepsake

Kiss

Labor of love

Lace

Lavish

Leading ladies

License

Lifetime

Limo

Live in love

Location

Look of love

Love

Love about town

Love affair

Love goes to town

Love hits the town

Love in the city…

Love is in the air…

Love on the run

Love story

Loves hits the town!

Luminous pearls

Mad about you...

Mad about...

Made for each other

Made in heaven

Maid in heaven

Maid of honor

Main event

Mane

Mane event

Married in the metropolitan

Match made in heaven

Matchmaker

Meant to be

Melt with you

Memorable moments

Modern romance

Moment to remember

Moments

Mon amour

Monogram

Moonstruck in Manhattan

Moonstruck in the city

Most memorable day of your life

Mr. & Mrs.

Obsessed

Obsession

Open bar

Palette

Pearls

Perfect match

Perfect pastels

Photographer

Pick your palette

Placemats

Promise

Reception

Remember

Ribbons

Ring

RSVP

Save the date

Say "I do"

Say "Yes"

Season's soirees

Set your heart on…

Sheer joy

Sneak peek

Soft spot

Something blue

Something borrowed

Something new

Special delivery

Start planning

Start swooning…

Straight from your heart

Stunner

Stunning

Sweetheart

Swoon in the city

Talk of the town

That's amore!

That's love

The big day

This time it's love

This way to…

Tiered/tiers

Tiers of joy

To have and to hold

Toast

Toast of the town

Together forever

Train

True romance

Unforgettable

Unforgettable moments

Unity

Unveiled

Updo

Usher

Venue

Vision in white

Vow to…

Vows

We love weddings

Wedding belles

Wedding bells

Wedding of your dreams

Wedding party

Wedding tradition

Wedding-worthy

White

White hot

Winter wedding bliss

Winter wedding wonderland

Winter whites…

Yes!

You're cordially invited

Your presence is requested

*For more inspiration, see **Valentine's Day** on pg 70.

SECTION 6:

HOME AND DÉCOR

BATH

Ahhhhh…

All washed up

Bath and body works

Bath beauties

Bath time

Bath time beauties

Bathe

Bathing beauties

Breezy

Bright

Bubble trouble

Bubbles

Clean

Clean break

Clean conscience

Clean slate

Clean start

Clean sweep

Clean up

Clean up your act

Clean freak

Clean-cut

Come clean

Daily routine

Dry off

Fresh and clean

Fresh start

Good clean fun

Hot bath

Just add water

Lather up!

Lather. Rinse. Repeat.

Make a splash

Makin' a splash

Makin' waves

Master bath

Medicine cabinet

Medicine cabinet makeover

Neat freak

Powder room

Primp

Refresh

Rub a dub

Shower power

So fresh and so clean

Soak

Soak up spring!

Spa

Spa day

Splish, splash

Spring

Spring clean your bath

Spring clean-up!

Spring cleaning

Spruce up

Squeaky clean

Suds, bubbles

Sunny & sheer

Take a bath

The ultimate spring awakening

Time to come clean!

Top shelf

Tub time

Under-the-sink space

Washing space

Water baby

Wet 'n' wild

BEDROOM AND BEDDING

Beauty sleep

Bedding bliss

Best of bedding

Best bedding buys

Bedding blitz

Bright, happy bedding

Cloud-like

Come out of hibernation

Cover up

Deep sleep

Don't sleep on it

Dream bedding

Dream come true

Dream on

Dream ticket

Dream world

Hibernate

Hit the snooze button

Impossibly soft

Layer it on

Layers of …

Make your bed

Pile on the style

R&R

Return to slumber

Serenity now

Sleep cycle

Sleep easy

Sleep in

Sleep on it

Sleep tight

Sleeping sanctuary

Snuggle in

Snuggle up to…

Suite dreams

Sweet dreams

Wake up on the bright side

We've got you covered

Wrap up

You snooze you lose

GO GREEN

…does a world of good	Earth to [firstname]
A bold step forward	Earth-friendly
All-natural…	Earth-gentle
Au natural	Earth-loving
Back to nature	Earth-smart
Be good to the earth	Earth-wise
Better nature	Easy on the earth
Bold by nature	Eco
Bold in nature	Eco-bedding
Bold strokes in organic	Eco-boost
By nature	Eco-chic
Call of nature	Eco-chick
Certified organic	Eco-cotton
Clean	Eco-first
Clean living	Eco-friendly
Conscious living	Eco-gentle
Course of nature	Eco-luxe
Do your part	Eco-maniac
Earth angel	Eco-minded
Earth first	Eco-power

Eco-retreat

Eco-smart

Ecotourism

Environmental responsibility

Ethical

Extreme green

Fair trade

For life

Forces of nature

Future generations

Gentle cotton

Gentle organics

Get green

Give the green light

Go all out with organic

Go green

Good for the earth and you

Good natured

Good to the earth and you

Green

Green beat

Green energy

Green for life

Green house

Green living

Green means go!

Green with envy

Green-wise

Greensmart

Guilt-free

Higher standards

It's your world

Keen on green

Livegreen

Make every day earth day

Mother earth

Mother nature

Natural

Natural beauty

Natural science

Natural wonder

Naturally bold

Nature in focus

Non-toxic

Organic

Organic chemistry

Organic matters

Recycle your pile

Reduce, reuse, recycle

Renewable resources

Responsible

Return to nature

Second nature

Seeing green

Sleep green

Small footprints

Sustainable

True to nature

Waste-free

World-wise

Zero waste

FURNITURE DESCRIPTORS

Accented with…

Aged bronzed-iron frame

All in the accents

Americana

Artisan-crafted

Beachside bungalow

Bohemian

Boho meets modern

Botanical boho

Bun feet

Classic country farmhouse

Coastal

Coastal chic

Coastal retreat

Contemporary

Cozy chic

Craftsman's attention to detail

Danish modern

Detailed with

Distinctive

Eclectic

Elaborate moldings

English country

Farmhouse finds

Feminine farmhouse

Flea market finds

Free-spirited

French boho

French country…

Furniture favorite

Gritty chic

Hand-carved

Handcrafted

Industrial

Industrial modern

Luxe loft

Mid-century

Midcentury modern

Minimalist

Modern industrial

Modern military

Modern mosaic

Modern rustic

Nautical style

Original design

Plushly padded

Rethink rustic

Rustic

Rustic farm charm

Rustic farmhouse

Rustic-chic

Scandinavian

Seaside style

Shabby chic

Ski chalet

Southwestern sensibility

Steampunk

Traditional

Tropical oasis

Twisted columns

Weathered finish

Whip-stitching

GARDENING

A little dirt don't hurt

A tree is born

April showers

Au natural

Bed of roses

Bumper crop

Can you dig it?

Cherry-pick

Cream of the crop

Crop up

Dig deep

Dig in

Dig it

Dig your heels in

Digging

Dirty work

Down and dirty

Early bloomer

Flower patch

Flower power

Flower tools

Garden tools

Garden variety

Get to the root of it

Get your hands dirty

Go green

Green space

Green thumb

Green with envy

Grow your garden

Here's the dirt

In the weeds

Late bloomer

Mow, blow and go

Nature calls

Petal power

Plant a seed

Planting

Play dirty

Plenty of sunshine

Roll up your sleeves

Secret garden

Spring showers

Talk dirty

Tool up

Tools of the trade

Turn over a new leaf

Watching plants grow

Watering

Weed out

Weeding

You plant a seed

You reap what you sow

*For more inspiration, see
Florals on pg 12.

LIGHTING

All aglow!

At first light

Beam

Bright

Bright delights!

Bright direction

Bright idea

Bright light

Bright lights in sight

Brighten up

Brighten your…

Brilliant idea

Bring to light

Cast a glow

Dim down

Dim up

Don't be in the dark

Evening glow

Flash

Flip a switch

Get the halo

Gleaming

Glow

Glow & behold!

Glow a long way

Glow ahead

Glow for it

Glow on

Glow with it

Go for the glow

Hello glow

Hello, halo

High shine

Illuminate

Illuminating

In glowing colors

In glowing terms

In light of…

It's glow time!

Let there be light

Lights we love

Light bright

Light it right

Light it right up!

Light up

Light up any corner

Light up the night

Light up your life

Lightshow

Lit

Look on the bright side

Morning glow

Oh so bright!

Outshine

Ray of light

Ready, set, glow

Ring of light

Rise and shine

Say watt?

See the light

Shed some light on...

Shimmer

Shine

Shine bright

Shine on

Shining example

Sparkle

Steal the spotlight

Switch off

Switch on

Take a shine to...

Take your ... in the bright direction

The right light

This ... is lit

Turn on

Turn up

Watts in it for you?

Watts up?

MIRRORS

Be on the lookout

Dirty looks

Don't look back

Don't look now, but…

Double take

Eyeing something…

First look

Keep a watch on…

Look ahead

Look closer

Look forward

Look here!

Look it up!

Look me up

Look on the bright side

Look sharp

Look the other way

Look the part

Look, mirrors!

Lookin' good

Looking glass

Looking high & low

Mirror, mirror

On watch

Outlook

Picture

Reflect on

Reflect upon

Reflect your style

See yourself

Shine

Sparkling mirrors that outshine the sun

Sunny outlook

Take a look at…

Take another look

Watch out

We looked high and low

RUGS

Anchor your space

Art underfoot

Be floored

Best foot forward...

Cover your floors with color

Cushion your feet

Floor-ever!

Floor-friendly layers

Foot traffic

Hand-loomed

Lay out some style

Loom or bust

More for your floor

Natural fibers

Pile it on

Pile style

Pull the carpet/rug

Put your foot down

Roll out our best rugs

Rugrats

Rug rollout

Shag rugs

Step into style

Step it up

Step on it!

Step out...

Step to it

Step up your style

Style-packed rugs

Sweep under the rug

Take the floor

Treat your feet

Tufted rugs

SEATING AND CHAIRS

Best chairs in the house

Best seat in the house

Bottom's up

Can we show you to your seat?

Chair-y good

Comfort from the bottom up

Comfort seat

Cuddle for two

Don't sit this out

Find your comfort zone

Front-row seats

Grab a chair

Hours in the saddle

Live & let lounge

Live for lounging

Live the lounge life

Live, love, lounge

Long live lounge

Lounge act

Lounge like you mean it

Lounge solo

Please be seated

Pledge your love for lounge

Power seat

Pull up a chair

Pull up a seat

Ringside seats

Saved you a seat

Seat of power

Sit down for this

Sit pretty

Sitting pretty

Southern comfort

Swoon-worthy seating

Take a load off

Take a seat

Take your seats

The bottom line

True to form

SHARED SPACES

A match made to last

A shared space means twice the style

Classic harmony

Double down

Double duty

Double take

Double the style

Double trouble

Double up

Double your style in a shared space

Great minds think alike

Make it match for…

Make your match

Matching

Meet your match

Mix and match

Paired up

Perfect pair

Seeing double

Share your space

Share your style

Sharing

Stylish solutions for shared spaces

Share with twice the style

Synchronize your…

Take two

Together

Twice as nice

Twice the style

Twinsies

Two is better than one

STORAGE AND ORGANIZATION

A happy home

A place for everything

A simple, smart, storage-friendly space

Basket case

Big ideas for small spaces

Bins to bookcases

Bins, buckets, baskets

Clean-sweep

Clear out

Coat closet chaos

Color coding

Conquer clutter

Contain everything

Contain yourself

Corral your stuff

Decluttering hacks

Decluttering routine

Designated area(s)

Double your space

Downsize

Fight future clutter

File it away

Find what you're looking for in no time

Free yourself from clutter

Get a jump on…

Get in a zone

Get organized

Go from to-do to all done

Hide cord clutter

Hide your cords

Highly classified

Hold everything

Hot mess

Keep things neat

Kick clutter to the curb

Let's get organized

Manage your media center

Master the mess

Modular mix

Multitasking

New Year resolution

Organize this

Organized mess

Organizing essentials

Out of control

Out of sight

Plan it out'

Pro tip

Quick storage solutions

Resolution solutions

Resolve to get organized

Save some space

Save space

Shelf it!

Small-space solutions

Smart and easy

Sort and edit

Sort it out

Stash it all

Stay organized

Storage hacks

Storage that packs a punch

Storage-packed

Stow your…

Sweep aside

Sweep away

Sweep up

Tackle your…

Take inventory

Take stock

Take your list from "to-do" to "all done"

Time-saver

Total closet bliss

Wanted: More storage

Well-organized home

Wrangle your…

WINDOWS

A better room in view

Be on the lookout

Bright ideas in…

Change your view

Creative with curtains

Curtain call

Don't close the window on…

Don't miss your window

Double take

Drape expectations

Dress your windows

Entire/complete lineup

Go to great lengths

Great drapes

Hang up some color/style

Here comes the sun...

Improve your view

In view

Go window-shopping

Layer sheers and panels

Look ahead to…

Look forward to [season]

Look on the bright side

Look out for…

Outlook

Pair sheers & panels

Point of view

Pull it together (curtains)

Pulled-together look

Ray of light

Rosy outlook

Shades of spring / summer / winter / fall

Shine

Sun in sight

Sunny outlook

Sunny updates

Sunny-day style

Treat your windows

Wake up your windows

Window of opportunity

Window shopping?

Windows that wow

Windows upgrade

You've opened the
window on…

SECTION 7:

MISCELLANEOUS MARKETING MESSAGES

ABANDON CART

Can you watch my stuff?

Decisions, decisions…

Don't you forget about me

Give it another look…

I want you to want me

Is this yours?

Just looking around?

Looks like you left
something behind…

Need help deciding?

Ready to check out?

Still thinking it over?

Take another look…

Thanks for visiting, but you
left something behind

These might also work
for you…

We put these aside for you…

We're watching your stuff…

We've got your items…

We've saved your
shopping cart

What do you think about
these?

You left something behind…

You left it in your
shopping bag

Your shopping cart is safe
with us

Your stuff is safe with us

ADJECTIVES

Aloha-inspired

Authentic

Bigger is better (and comfier!)

Billowing

Boho

Bold

Bold

Breezy

Brilliant

Catch the eye

Charming

Chic

Classic

Color-drenched patterns

Color-rich

Complex

Confident/confidence

Cozy

Cozy relaxed fit…

Crafty

Crisp

Cute and flirty

Delicate

Deluxe

Downtown

Downtown cool

Drapey

Durable

Eclectic

Exclusive

Extreme

Floppy

Fresh

Funky fun

Genuine

Graceful

Heirloom

High performance

High-end

Illuminating

Ingenious

Innovative

Laidback

Life-size/larger-than-life

Lush

Luxury

Magnetic

Multifunctional

Natural texture and dimension
(for rugs or eco-friendly
things)

Oversized

Plush

Posh

Precision

Preppy

Relaxed

Roomy, comfy,

Rugged

Sculptural silhouette

Sharp

Slouchy

Smart

Soft – cozy – comfy – cushy –
silky – velvety

Soft 'n' slouchy

Solid

Sophisticated

Sporty

Stout

Strong

Sturdy

Supersized

Supersoft

Sweet

Sweet & playful

Taste of the tropics

The only ... you need to own

Tough

Trendy

Tropical-themed

Ultimate

Vibrant

Well-built

Wonderful

CONVERSATIONS

(Okay, maybe not.)

Admit it, you're just
as obsessed

Ah-ma-zing

Ahh yeah…

Am I right?

And we just had to show
off these…

Are you ready for this?

Awesome!

Can you handle it?

Can't keep our hands
off these…

Can't wait.

Check it out.

Cuh-razy

Don't you just love when…

Fabulous!

Finally!

Fired up!

Game on!

Get out of here!

Get out!

Get pumped

Goody!

Hello, …

Here's the deal

Here's the scoop

Hey

Hey everyone…

Hey you with the...

Hooray!

How cute are these?

It's about to go down

Let's hang

No big deal

No prob

Not your type? No prob.

Oh these?

Oh this?

OMG!

On a roll

Pretty amazing

Pretty awesome

Psst…yeah, you!

Really!

Right on!

Score

Seals the deal

See ya soon

Seriously

So crazy, right?

So down with…

So into…

So, here's the sitch…

So, we found the … of your dreams.

Sweet!

This rocks!

Tight!

To seal the deal…

Trust us, your … will thank you

Truth be told

We got this

We see you

We'll keep this short…

We're not messin'

We're not playing games (but you probably will be)

We're obsessed.

What's up

Woohoo!

Woot!

Yay!

Yeah, baby!

Yes!

Yippee!

You bet

You betcha

You can freak out now…

You need these.

You owe it to yourself to check this out

You will not believe

You'll be hooked…

You'll want to see this…

You're welcome.

MAKING MEMORIES

Affair to remember

Indelible

Indelible experiences

Indelible memories

Last a lifetime

Lasting impressions

Lasting memories

Lasting moments

Lifelong memories

Lifetime of memories

Look back on…

Make memories

Memorable

Memories new and old…

Memories that last

Memory of a lifetime

Never forget

One to remember

Recall

Recollect

Reconnect over new memories

Reflect on…

Relive

Relive shared memories

Remember

Remember for years to come

Remembrances

Reminder…

Reminisce

Reminiscence

Unforgettable

NEW

A new spin on…

A new take on an old…

A whole new…

An updated…

Arrivals

At last, they're here!

Better than new

Brand new

Brand spanking new

Brave new world

Come see your new…

Crowd pleasers

Dreaming of a new…?

Exciting new…

Favorites

Finally! New collections for…

Find your new favorites

For a look that's entirely new!

Fresh new…

Here they are!

Hot off the wire

Ideas

Introducing: The latest and greatest from…

It's all new

Just in

Looks

May we introduce you to our new…?

Must-haves

New arrivals

New collections are here!

New essentials

New kid on the block

New school

New solutions

New standard

New this month/week…

New!

Newest

No more waiting! Our…
collections are here

Our latest hits

Over XX new…

Ready for a change?

Recent arrivals

Say goodbye to…;
say hello to…

Say hello to…

See what's new at…

Styles

They're here! All-new
collections

Updates

What's new?

What's new? Our latest (and
greatest) collections

Whole new ballgame

You haven't seen these yet…

PERSONALIZATION

…get(s) personal

100s of ways to make it yours

A more personalized…

Add your name or initials
to these …

Add your name to these…

All your own

Be unique

Brand your … better!

Bringing personalization into
focus

Create your own look

Customize it

Customize your … with
your …

Design your own.

Don't just give a…;
Give a keepsake.

First-name basics

Get personal

Give a gift that stands out

Give a personalized keepsake

Give signature gifts and style

Have it your way

Initial impression

It's all in a name

Make your gifts personal

Uniquely yours…

Personally speaking

It's all yours

Just add your name!

Leave a lasting
impression with
personalization

Leave a mark

Made for them

Made to order

Make a name for yourself

Make it yours

Make our collections
your own

Make things personal

Make your … stand out with
customized …

Make your gift the one that
stands out

Make your mark with
personalized gifts

Making … more personal

Name your bedding

One of a kind

One-of-a-kind designs

Our collections, your name

Our pieces. Your design.

Our styles, your design.

Personalization in the
spotlight

Personalize it!

Personalize our pieces

Personalize your … with your
name/initials

Personalized gifts to give
and get

Spotlight on: Personalization

To the letter

You found it! The perfect
personalized gift

You make it you

You name it

You're the designer

Your design

Yours truly

POWER

XX ways to boost your…

Accelerate

Accelerated

Advanced

Bolster

Boost

Boost up

Boost your…

Could your … use a boost?

Dare to think bigger

Efficient

Elevate

Enrich

Extra power boost

Flex your muscle

Flex your power

Give your … the ultimate
power boost

Improve

Increase

Maximize

More power to you!

Performance

Power boost

Power trip

Power up!

Strength

The edge

Ultimate … booster

Ultimate power boost

Ultra power play

Upgrade

PRODUCTIVITY / PERFORMANCE

… means fewer interruptions and more productivity

24 hours a day

Add more productivity

All access

Any time

Around the clock

Be more efficient with…

Be more productive with…

Better performance

Boost productivity

Command performance

Competitive streak

Daily productivity

Do more…

Get back to work fast

Get it all done

Get everything done

Get more done

Get more done in a day

Get more done in less time

Gets the job done

Goal-oriented

Increase productivity

Make fast work of…

No interruptions

Nonstop

Outperforms the competition

Productivity boost

Save time and get back to work fast

Time is money. Save both with…

Without interruptions

Won't quit

Work more efficiently with…

Work without interruption

Works immediately

Your work is never interrupted

RATINGS AND REVIEWS

Add your voice to the mix

Alright, let's hear it…

Did you laugh? Cry? Scratch your head?

Did you love it?

Do you love it?

Don't keep us in suspense

Have you read these reviews?

Have you seen these rave reviews?

Help others find the perfect…

Help others find the right…

Help your fellow … fans find the perfect … by reviewing your recent purchases

Hip, hip, hooray for rave reviews

Is it love or a dud?

Join the conversation by sharing a review

Look what's scoring rave reviews…

Love your purchase?

Love your purchase? Let us know!

Nothing makes us happier than making our customers happy

Nothing makes us happier than when our customers are happy

Now that you've gotten to know your latest purchase…

People/Customers rave about this…

Rate and review your purchases

Rate your purchases and spread the word

Rating your product only takes a moment

Rave reviews

Ready to review your recent purchase?

Review your latest purchase now

Review your recent purchases now

Share with other … fans.

So, what do you think?

Spread the word

Spread the word by rating
your purchases

Submit your review

Tell us what you think…

Thanks for your purchase.
Ready to review?

The reviews are in!

We love that our customers
love us

We want to hear what
you think

We'd love to hear what
you think!

We'd love to hear your
thoughts (and so would other
customers)

We'd love to hear
your thoughts

We're dying to know

Would you recommend
it to others?

Write a review!

Your fellow … fans will
thank you!

TIME

Around the clock

At the speed of business

Be efficient

Crunch time

Deadline?

Do more for less

Do more than before

Don't waste time

Expedite

Express

Fast-paced

Faster than ever

Faster than you ever imagined

Fastest turnaround

Final hours

Full speed ahead

Get the most time-saving
tricks

High time

How much is your
time worth?

In no time

In nothing flat

In the nick of time

Increase your speed

It's... – only faster

It's a real timesaver

Just in time

Maximize time

More time on work, less time
on paperwork

More time-saving tricks.

Need for speed

Need something STAT?

No time to kill

No time to lose

Now with more
time-saving tricks

On time, all the time

Out of time

Pick up the pace

Race against the clock

Race against time

Reduce time

Right on time

Same-day

Save (even more) time

Save more time

Save time in your day and
money in pockets

Save time, money – and
your sanity

Save time, money and the day!

Save time, save money, save
your sanity

Send it STAT

Speed up

Speedy

Speedy, secure, simple

Spend less time

Take the time

Time flies

Time is money

Time is of the essence

Time is on your side

Time of your life

Time-saver

Time-saving solutions

Time's ticking…

Total timesaver

Turn A.S.A.P into N.B.D.
(no big deal)

Turn C.O.B. into A.S.A.P.

Who couldn't use more time?

Work faster, save more time

Your time (and money)
are valuable

SOCIAL MEDIA

All the places you can find us

Are we friends yet?

Are you social?

Find us on…[social icons]

Go ahead, stalk us

Here's where you can find us

Join our social club

Keep up with us

Let's be more than friends

Let's get social

Let's hang…

More places to find us

Pass it on…

Share on…

Show it off

Social butterfly

Social scene

Socialize with us

Stalking is highly encouraged

Stay in touch throughout your journey

Want to be friends?

We encourage stalking.
(We don't mind.)

We like "likes"

We show off

We tweet back

We'd love for you to join us

Where to find us

UNLIMITED

... times unlimited!

All-in-one

All-inclusive

Anything's possible

Best value: unlimited...

Bottomless

Comprehensive

Get the ultimate

Get unlimited

Go big (like, really big) with unlimited...

Go big, go unlimited!

Go the limit!

How limitless is unlimited?

Limitless

Make the move to unlimited

Mission possible

No boundaries

No limitations

No limitations. No problems.

No limits

No limits, no problem

No restrictions

Ready to go unlimited?

The cloud's the limit

The sky's the limit

The ultimate in...

The ultimate plan for unlimited...

Ultimate plan for unlimited...

Ultimate, unlimited...

Unleash

Unleash unlimited...

Unlimit your...

Unlimit yourself

Unlimited access

Unlimited access for limitless success

Unlock unlimited...

Work without limits

You could have unlimited...

SECTION 8:

NUMBERS

NUMBERS GAME

…and counting

At first count

At last count

But who's counting

By the number

Count off

Count out

Countdown

Crunch numbers

Cushy number

Days are numbered

Dial your digits

Do a number on…

Do the digits

Do the numbers

Exchange numbers

Grand sum

Grand total

Hidden figures

Hot number

In total

Keep count

Lose count

Number cruncher

Number is up

Out for the count

Safety in numbers

Score your digits

Take a number

Total

Total up

Wrong number

TWO / DOUBLE

…strikes twice!

…times two!

A double dose

Couple up

Dare you to grab two

Do a double take

Double dating

Double down

Double header

Double knockout

Double or nothing

Double play!

Double take

Double up

Double your...

Get into two

Gimme two!

Go ahead, go for seconds

I'll take two

Make do with two

Make it a double

Make it a pair

Make it two

More fun than one!

On the double

Once bitten, twice buy

One's never enough

Pair off!

Pair up

Perfect pair

Seeing double

Total two-timer

Twice as...

Twice the...

Twin set

Two's company

Two looks in one

Two, please!

Two times the charm

Two-timer!

Two's company

Two's the trick...

You deserve two

You need two...

You, times two

TWO FOR ONE / DOUBLE

2 for 1

Buy 2 for the price of one

Buy a year, and we'll give you a year free

Buy a year, get a year free

Buy one, get one free

Buy your first, and the second is on us

Double your…

Double your dollar

Get two for half the price

Giving away one free

Half off

Half price

It takes two

More fun than one

On the double

Twice as nice

Two for one!

Two for the price of one

Two-for-one deal

Two-for-one special

THREE/TRIPLE

3D

Third

Third degree

Third eye blind

Third-hand

Third-kind

Third-party

Third-person

Third wheel

Third-world

Three men & a baby

Three musketeers

Three sheets to the wind

Three stooges

Three times the…

Three-way

Three-ring circus

Three's company

Triad

Trifecta

Trio

Triple

Triple threat

Triplets

Trois

FOUR

4 ever

4 real

Four corners

Four score

Four sheets

Four-letter word

On all fours

What's the 4-1-1

FIVE

9 to 5

Gimme five

Hang five

High-five

Take five

Take the fifth

TEN

10 out of 10

Hang ten

Take ten

Ten-four

Total ten

SECTION 9:

PEOPLE

FAMILY

A house divided

All in the family

Baby blues

Baby fever

Bloodlines

Brother from another mother

Different strokes for different folks

Extended family

Family affair

Family business

Family circle

Family crest

Family dinner

Family dollar

Family feud

Family fun

Family guy

Family history

Family jewels

Family man

Family matters

Family outing

Family ties

Family tree

Family vacation

Family values

Find your tribe

Grow your family

Home folks

Immediate family

It runs in the family

It takes a village

Kid gloves

Kids will be kids

Like father, like son

Meet our newest family member

New kid on the block

Not your father's…

Not your mother's…

One of the family

Runs in the family

Sibling rivalry

Sister from another mister

Soul brother

Soul sister

The kids are alright

The newest members of our family…add them to your family

We are family

We're growing our family

Welcome to the family!

Whizz kids

You're one of the family

Friends with benefits

Friends, family, fashion!

Just between friends…

Only the best for our friends…

Tell all your friends

We like to treat our friends…

You're on our list…

Your friends & fashion fix…

*For more inspiration, see **Sale and Promotions** on pg 135.

FRIENDS & FAMILY EVENTS

Because friends don't let friends miss out on…

For our friends, old and new!

For our most stylish friends…

Friends in chic places

SUPERHEROES

Ability

Absolute power

Action-packed

Archenemy

Backstory

Bam!

Battle

Be a hero

Boom!

Brave deeds and actions

Captain

Costumed heroes

Crime fighters

Divine powers

Empowered

Energize

Fall from power

Fly in

Flying high

Full speed

Gadgets

Good vs. evil

In a flash

Kapow!

Kick

Knowledge is power

Kryptonite

Legends

More power to you!

Myths

Packs a punch

Pow!

Power

Power play

Power trip

Power up…

Power-packed

Save the day

Secret identity

Secret weapons

Shield

Speedy

Splat!

State-of-the-art technology

Strength

Super-villains

Superhero

Superheroine

superhuman

Supernatural

Superspeedy

Teleport

Threats against humanity

To the rescue

Ultimate power play

Universe

Unsung hero

Weaknesses

With great power comes great
responsibility

Wonder

Zap!

Zip!

TEENS

'Bout it

'Sup hottie?

'tude

faints

sighs

100% spring break!

A-list

Addicted

Admit it, you're just as obsessed…

Afterhours

Ah-ma-zing

All-nighter

Am I your type?

Amaaazing

Another all-nighter

Attitude

Awesome

Awesomely cute

Babes

Be mine

Best ever

Besties

Bling

Boogie

Book report

Bring it on

Bring the gang

Bring the whole crew

Buzz

Can't wait!

Chat soon!

Check it out…

Check me out

Check you out

Chica

Cool your jets

Crazy

Crazy amazing

Crush

Cuh-razy

Cuh-ute

Cutest couple

Cutie

Decked out

Dig it

Dish

Don't you just love?

Dream on

Drool much?

Effortlessly cool

Fave

Find your perf shade

Fired up

Flirty

Freaking out

Gather your crew

Get a lil crazy

Get a load of…

Get hooked

Get in line…

Get into it…

Get pumped!

Get the deets

Get wild

Glam

Glitter

Got me trippin'

Gym

Heart this!!

Heartthrob

Here's my number…

Here's the sitch…

Hey everyone!

Hit on this

Home girl

Hot for…

Hot looks

Hot mess

Hot stuff

Hot, hot, hot

Hotties

How cute are these?

Hype

I got this…

I gotta bug

I gotta motor

I'm digging it

I'm pumped

In heaven

In your dreams

Insane

Insanely cute

Instant [noun/adjective]

Into it!

It's my jam

Jetsetter

Jump around

Kiss off

Lay it on me

Let's get this party started…

Let's hang

LOL

Lotsa love

Love

Love me some…

Luv it

Mad about…

Main squeeze

Major babe

Major score!

Major win

Make it hot…

Make the first move

Matchmaker

Most popular

Must-have

My pad

My place or yours?

My turn!

New girl alert

No big deal

No biggie

No filter

No prob

Obsessed

Okay, boomer

Omg

On-trend

Party 'til we see the sun

Party line

Party on!

Party-goers

Peace

Phenomenal

Pick me up

Pile on the …

Pretty amazing

Pretty perfect

Pronto

Pump it up!

Put it down like {name}

Ride with me…

Rock it!

Scoop

Score!

Serious buzz, serious love

Sleep in

Sleepin' in

Smokin'

Snap it up/snap 'em up

So crazy, right?

So cute

So into you

So loving this

So not my type

So perfect

Splash

Stellar

Sugar

Super cool

Super cute

Sweet escape

T.M.I.

Take me away

Teacher's pet

The lowdown

Totally

Totes

Totes love

Turn it up

Ultimate

Up all night

Vacay

VSCO girl

Wakey wakey!

Way, way cute

We're pumped

We're so down with this…

We're stoked

We're totally freaking
out over…

We're weak for…

What's up

What's up, cutie?

What's your damage?

Whoa!

Why not?

Wild ride

Work it!

Wow!

Xoxoxo

You can freak out now

You have got to see

You made the team

You snooze you lose

You'll flip

You're in

You're on the team

You're so fine

Your crew

Your gang

Your posse

Your room

SECTION 10:

SALE AND PROMOTIONS

CALL TO ACTION (CTA)

Be awesome >

Buy it now >

Celebrate >

Check it out >

Click here >

Connect >

Details >

Dig into… >

Discover >

Discover… >

Enroll >

Enter >

Enter for the chance to win >

Enter now >

Enter today >

Explore >

Get it free >

Get it now >

Get started >

Get the scoop >

Get yours free >

Give it a try >

Go >

Go now >

Go there >

Here's how >

How it works >

Join now >

Join the club >

Journey >

Learn more >

Let's do it >

More >

Plan >

Read >

Reserve >

Reserve a/an… >

Reserve my… >

Reserve your… >

RSVP >

Schedule >

See how it works >

See it in action >

See more >

Send a… >

Share your date >

Shop >

Shop now >

Show me how >

Show me my… >

Sign up – it's free! >

Sign up now >

Start now >

Start your trial >

Talk to us >

Try it free >

Try it now >

Uncover >

Watch >

DEAL OF THE DAY/WEEK

…of the week

12 days of…

12 days of cheer!

12 days of deals

12 days of goodies

12 days of real style, real steals

12 days of stellar steals

12 days of style

12 days of style steals

7-day deal

7-day special

7-day steal

7-day steal & save

7-day style steal

A new deal a day!

A new steal a day!

Chic steal of the day

Chic steal of the week

Daily dish

Drop in for a new deal every day!

In-the-spotlight steal

Must-see steal

Never miss a deal – stop by every day!

New steals every day

Oh, what fun! A new deal a day.

Our gift to you: A new deal a day!

Our stellar deal of the week

Our weekly steal

Shop a new sale every day

Shop 'til you drop…

Spotlight steal

Steal of the week

The save of the day

The weekly hit

The weekly score!

Unwrap a new steal every day

Weekly break

Weekly catch

Weekly steal

Weekly style steal

What's on special?

FREE SHIPPING

And don't miss free shipping

Bag free shipping

Be a showoff with
free shipping

Click quick! Get free shipping
while it lasts

Extra! Extra! Get free
shipping on select items

Extra! Extra! More free
shipping

Free delivery on…

Free shipping has arrived

Free shipping is just a
click away…

Free shipping on…

Get your gifts on time and
under the tree FREE

Give big with free shipping!

Great … that ship free

Hung up on free shipping?

Hurry up for free (holiday)
delivery

Love free shipping?

More free shipping!

On the house!

Rush ship your gifts

Save more with free shipping

Save on shipping on more
than … items

Save with free shipping on
select items

See more than … items that
ship free!

Shiny new … with free ship

Ship more … FREE

Shipping? It's on the house.

Shop free shipping (with no
minimum order)

Skip shipping fees

Special delivery: free shipping!

Stay home. Shop online. Ship
your gifts free!

The best … ship free!

The shipping's free on over …
items

The shipping's free!

The shipping's on us for
over ... items.

The shipping's on us!

To your house, on the house

Want more free shipping?

Want more savings? Shop free
shipping

We ship it quick and for free

We'll deliver the goods
for free

We'll deliver them for free!

We're showing off more
free shipping

Why pay for shipping?

Wrap it up early with
free shipping

XX+ gifts with free ship

Zip in for free shipping

IN STORES ONLY

Be our guest…

Breeze in…

Definitely worth stopping for…

Drop everything & drop by…

Drop in for xx% off your entire in-store purchase

Enjoy XX% off everything in stores…but not for long!

Good things are in store

Good things are in store and online

In store and now online

In-store exclusive

Make a visit

Now in stores (but not for long)

Only for our guests…

Only in store, only for a limited time

Only in stores!

Our best guests…

Our sale is only in store.

Pop in for…

Pop in sometime

See a list of stores and galleries around the world

See it in person

See it in store

Stop by & say hi!

Stop by a store

Stop by sometime!

Stop by, save big

Stop by. Say hi. Save big.

Stop, look, shop!

There's more in store…

Visit us

Want to see it in person?

Want to stop by?

We're treating our guests to XX% off

What's in store?

Worth stopping for: xx% off your in-store purchase!

XX% off in-store. Need we
say more?

You asked, we listened.

You're our guest of honor...

INTERNATIONAL

… goes global!

… is going places

… is universal

… knows no boundaries

1st class

A whole new world

A world of…

Across the world

All over the map

Around the globe

Because … knows no borders

Best of all worlds

Compass

Countries

Four corners of the earth

G.P.S.

Globetrotter

Going global

Going places

Good … knows no boundaries

Good … travels fast

International

It's a small world…

Jetsetter

Map

Map out

Miles to go…

No borders

No passport

Pack your bags

Passport to…

Put … on the map

Sharing … with the world

Special delivery

Spread the love

Taking … global

We're going places (to 000 countries to be exact)

World-class

*For more inspiration, see **Travel** on pg. 211.

LIMITED EDITION

1 of only X,XXX made

All new. So limited.

Collectible

Few and far between

Get it while it's hot

Gotta-have limited edition

Limited edition design

Limited edition must-have

Limited edition obsession

Limited edition! (Seriously.)

Limited exclusive!

Limited love

Limited original!

New (but only a few!)

New & exclusive

New & limited

New, original, limited

Oh-so limited!

Psst…it's limited edition!

Rare

Scarce quantities

Small run

So cute, oh-so limited!

So cute, so limited!

Special edition

LIMITED TIME + URGENCY

…are being carried away fast

…are flying fast

Almost gone…

Almost over

Before it's gone

Big savings, limited quantities

Booking fast

But not for long

But only for a limited time

But only until…

By invite only…

Clearing out

Click fast, these savings won't last

Click quick, these deals are going fast

Did you forget?

Did you hear?

Don't lose out

Don't lose your stuff…

Don't miss it

Don't miss out

Don't miss the boat

Don't miss the party

Don't sleep on it!

Don't wait

Ends soon

Ends tonight

Flying fast

Flying off the shelves

Going, going, today's the last day!

Going, going…

Gone in a flash

Here today, gone tomorrow!

Hurry…

If you snooze, you lose

It all ends tonight

It's here (finally!)

It's here! (but not for long…)

It's nearly over

It's not too late

It's now or never!

It's your last chance

Last day

Limited-time savings too good to last!

No time to wait!

Oh no! Don't miss it

Pick up your favorites fast

Race

Run, don't walk

Rush

Rushing off

Save your heart out

Seize the day!

Shop your heart out

Snag your favorites fast

So little time, so much to save.

Still on…but not for long.

Still time, but not much

The sale disappears in 3, 2, 1

There's still time

These go quickly, so hurry

This is huge

This is it

Today & online only

Today's the day!

Today's your last chance

Today's your last day

Tonight's the night.

Too good to last

Use it or lose it!

Vanishing fast…

What are you waiting for?

While you still can

Won't last…

You're about to miss out

Your last chance…

Your promo code ends tonight!

Your promo code expires at midnight

GET IT FIRST

Be the first

Before anyone else

Early access

Exclusive invite: Be the first

First come, first served

First dibs

First in line

First look

First pick

First take

Get 'em first!

Get 'em here first!

Get a first look

Jump in first

Love at first peek

Love at first sight

Love at first sneak peek

Shop first!

Shop it before anyone else

Shop it one week early

Shop now and get first pick

You first!

You go first!

You heard it here first

You saw 'em here first

You're the first to know

SALE

A+ finds

At a fraction of the cost…

Been waiting for a sale?
This is the one!

Best bet

Best buy

Best deal

Best savings are always at a
clearance

Bigger, better sale!

Brilliant buys

Chic styles, chic prices

Class picks

Cost-saving

Cut your costs

Deal steals

Did someone say clearance?

Don't miss it

Dream deals

Easy on your budget

Extra, Extra: New styles
added!

Extra! Extra!

Fill your home for less

Flawless finds at perfect prices

Fresh new savings for…

Fresh new styles just added…

Get it or regret it

Get ready for one stellar sale

Get ready for some
serious shopping

Go ahead, indulge

Going on now

Good thing you waited

Got a list? Get it now.

Happening now…

Help us clean house…

How much will you save?

Hurry in…

It's on!

Know why we love clearances?

Layer on the savings & style for fall!

Max out your style at a minimum price

Max style, mini price

Maximum style. Minimum price.

More for your money

More styles in the mix!

More styles, more sale!

More to fall for at the sale!

More, more, MORE styles added

Must-have super steals

Must-see savings

Must-see steals

New savings at the sale

Nice price

Now this is a sale!

Now's your chance to get everything

One low price

Our sale's on sale

Pays for itself

Perfect pieces, perfect prices

Rake in bigger savings…

Rake in these savings!

Ready, set, click

Ready, set, indulge

Ready, set, more sale!

Ready…set… sale!

Real steal

Save a bundle

Save on _____ costs

Save on what you crave

Save your company (and clients) money

Sayonara summer sale!

Sayonara summer, hello bigger savings!

Serious savings

Serious steals

Shiny new steals

Shop 'til you drop

Smart buy

Smart price

Smart steals

So long summer

Splendid styles, perfect prices

Steal the style

Stellar savings

Stellar steal

Stretch your dollar

Style steal

Super-style steals

Surprise: A bigger sale!

Surprise! Bigger savings
at the sale

Sweet steal

The IT sale

The So-Long-Summer Sale!

The styles you love…for less

There's more to shop
at the sale

This won't last long…

Too good to last…

Trust us, this is huge

Up to XX% off at the
clearance event

Waiting for a sale? This is it!

What have you had your eye
on? Get it now!

You're going to love this…

SEMI-ANNUAL SALE

Bigger, Better, Unbelievable

Everything you want…
and more!

Guilt-free shopping, on us!

It's here (finally!)

Love a good sale? This is it!

Ready. Set. Shop!

See it. Love it. Buy it!

The one you've been
waiting for.

The sale of all sales

The sale to splurge on!

The sale worth waiting for

This. Is. It!

Time to really seize the day

Your … will thank you!

SECTION 11:

SCHOOL AND WORK

BACK TO SCHOOL

[Mascot] Pride!

#1 fan

Ace your space!

Ahead of the class

All booked up

All day, all night

All for fall

Apply yourself

Attitude jersey

Back to class

Back to School 'XX

Back to school with…

Back to school, back to basics

Back to you…

Back-to-class essentials

Back-to-school basics

Back-to-school checklist

Biggest fan

Brainiac

Bringing the party

Cafeteria

Campus

Chalk it up

Chat

Cheat sheet

Class

Class picks

College confidential

Collegiate cool

Cool for school

Course loads

Credits

Crunch time

Crush the…

Crush those guys!

Do your thing

Don't be late

Don't be tardy

Dorm

Double major

E for effort

Extra credit

Extra points

Fall crush

Fall fever

Fall rush

Finally fall!

Fired up for fall

Five-minute break

Focus

Food fight

Fool 4 school

Fool for school

Friday night lights

Gameday tee

Game night

Game plan

Get it

Get it right

Get prepped

Give your … a wake-up call!

Go [team], go!

Go for the goal

Go get it

Hall pass

Hall-way patrol

Hallway traffic jam

Head of the class

Here to win!

Home room

Homework

Honor roll

Huddle

Keep it real

Kickstart your year

Let's do this

Let's pre-game

Lunch duty

Lunch menu

Makin' the grade…

Making tracks

Math & science

Mid-semester break

Morning bell!

Move-in must-haves

Multiple choice

My school rocks

My school rules

My school's better

New arrivals

New kid in class

New school

New-school gear

No loitering

No time like now…

Noteworthy

Now or never

Off campus

Off to school

On campus

Overachiever

Pennant

Pep rally

Playin' the field

Pledge

Pop quiz

Pregame

Prep rally

Prep's cool

Pumped up

Quad

Rally

Ready for Friday

Ready to rock

Ready to roll…

Ready, set, get it!

Ready. Set. Prep!/Pep!/Step!

Ring a bell

Roam the hallways

Rule the school

Rules of school

Rush

SATs

Saved by the…

Saved by the bell

School daze

School pride

School spirit

School zone

School's in session

Semester

Sharpen your pencils

Sign my yearbook

Ski break

Snack attack

Social studies

Spring break

Star student

State bound

Stomp

Study break basics

Study buddies

Study. Flirt. Sleep. Repeat.

Style's in session!

Summer break

Take home test

Take it outside

Team spirit

Team tee

Test your…

The best for back to school

Think outside of the (lunch)box

Time for social studies

True to you

Upgrade your space

Varsity blues

Wake-up call

Wake up to…

We're #1

What's for lunch

What's on the menu

Where's your spirit?

Winter break

With honors

Your best year ever

*For more inspiration, see **Graduation** on pg. 160.

COLLEGE / DORM

A-Z

After hours

After party

All-nighter

Alma mater

Best in show

Campus tour

Campus visit

Change your major

Class is out

College chic

College classic(s)

College confidential

Collegiate central

Collegiate cool

Cool for school tools

Cram session

Culture club

Deck out your dorm

Destination: Dorm

Dorm Basics 101

Dorm life

Double major

Double minor

Early decision

Extracurricular

Focus on studies

Fresh takes

Freshman, sophomore, junior, senior

Get schooled in…

Getting in

High scores

Hit the books

Home team

Hot topics

House party

Key dates

Lab group

Late-night study sessions

Lecture hall

Life in the dorms

Major: ...   Minor: ...

Make your dorm room the
ultimate hangout

Make your space the place
to be

Move-in must-haves

Off campus

Off to college

On campus

Reality check

Rock your school

School pride

School spirit

Stick by your school

Team spirit

Test your...

The new school supplies

The ultimate dorm room

Undergrad

Up all night

With honors

You're in.

Your best year yet!

Your dorm destination

Your school, your way!

IVY LEAGUE WORDS

Academic

Academy

All-American

Alma mater

Blazers

Boarding school

Born and bred

Brick & ivy

Campus

Class

Classic

College rule feel

Collegiate

Collegiate athletes

Crest

Hall pass

Hello, old sport

High standards

Higher learning

Hit the books,

Honors program

Hunter green

Institution

Ivy league

Ivy row

Jock-inspired

Lads

Legacy...

One for the team

Oxfords

Plaid

Polo

Prep school blues

Prep school cool

Prep style

Prep's cool

Preppy

Preppy & cool

Preppy collegiate

Private school

Rowing

Rugby

School of...

Set your own path

Social studies

Sophisticated yet casual

Step to prep

Study in style

Thorough bred

Tie

Top drawer

Traditional

Traditions

True prep

Uniform

University of...

Well-groomed

With honors

GRADUATION

Ahead of the curve

Announcements

Anything is possible

Be proud of yourself

Big dreams

Brave new world

Celebrate a great milestone

Ceremony

Cheers to the Class of 'XX

Cheers to you!

Class act

Class of 'XX

Commemorate this shining achievement

Commencement

Con-GRAD-ulations

Congratulate a graduate

Degree in hand

Diploma in hand

Display your diploma

Don't ever change

Embark on your next adventure

Get gifted for graduation

Gifts for grads

Going places

Good friends, good times

Goodbye dorm!

Grad school

Graduate picks

Graduate to your perfect …

Graduation invitations

Graduation party

Graduation pics

Graduation season

Graduation wishes

Great expectations

Hat's off!

Head of the class

Here's to you!

Here's to your future

In your future

It's your day

It's your move

Keys to success

Last day of class

Life's next chapter

Live and learn

Major milestone

Memorable

Never change

New direction

Oh, the places you'll go

On to the next adventure

On your own

Opportunity knocks

Overachiever

Pearls of wisdom

Powered up for success

Rad grads

Reach for the stars

School of hard knocks

School of life

School's out

School's out forever!

Sign my yearbook

Sky's the limit

Smart grads

So long study hall!

Tassel's worth the hassle

The next steps

The real world

The world is your oyster

Time of your life

To the nth degree

Top of the class

What lies ahead...

Words of wisdom

You did it!

You're going places

*For more inspiration, see
Back to School on pg. 153.

WORK

40-hour week

8 hours a day

9 to 5 and beyond

9 to 5 to happy hour

A bang up job

Above (one's) pay grade

All-hands meeting

Back in business

Barely getting by

Big wigs

Blue collar

Bonus

Business before pleasure

Business is business

Café to corner office

Clock in/out

Coffee run

Coffee talk

Corner office

Corner office to cocktail hour

Corporate job

Cubbies

Cup of ambition

Day job

Desk to dinner

Dirty jobs

Dirty work

Don't quit your day job

Fortune 100/500

From conference room to cocktail hour

From daytime to date night

Full-time job

Funny business

Get down to business

Get to work

Great job

Hard at work

Hardly working

Higher-ups

In and out of the office

In between gigs

It's not personal, it's business

Know your worth

Land a job

Leadership lessons

Lunch date

Make a living

Make it your business

Middle management

Monday meetings to Sunday brunch

Monkey business

Moonlighting

Morning meeting to happy hour

Move ahead

Net worth

Nice work

Nice work if you can get it

Odd jobs

Office gossip

Office or otherwise

On the hunt

One-to-one

Open for business

Out of office

Part-time job

Pay raise

Per my last email

Performance review

Pink collar

Place of business

Power lunch to Sunday brunch

Promotion

Quarterly earnings

Reply all

Right to work

Sick pay

Sleeping on the job

Startup environment

Strictly business

Strike pay dirt

The business of…

The hardest working person in
the office

To whom it may concern

Water cooler chat

Weekday to weekend

White collar

Work culture

Work from home

Work it out

Work overtime

Work remotely

Work to weekend

Work your way up

Work-to-weekend chic

Working hard

Working overtime

You've got work to do

SECTION 12:

SEASONS

WINTER

'tis the season

Ace the brisk temps

Apres all day

Apres ski

Arctic blast

At the heart of winter

Baby, it's cold outside

Beat the brrrr

Brave winter…

Brrrr-illiant

Brrrr…

Bundle up

Cabin fever

Chase the chill

Chill in

Cold comforts

Cold feet

Cold snaps

Cold spell

Cold wave

Cold-conquering…

Cold-weather…

Conquer the cold

Dashing through the snow

Extreme winter weather

First snow

Freeze warning

Freezing cold

Fresh powder

Frosty fantasy

Hit the slopes

Ice breakers

Ice over

Ice queen

Ice up

Ice, ice baby

Icy-cool

Keep cozy

Let it snow…

Oh, the weather outside is frightful

Ol' man winter

Outfox Jack Frost

Prep for powder

Sleigh the slopes

Snow bunny

Snow days

Snow inspo

Snowpocalypse

Stay in…

Sweater weather

The big chill

The most wonderful time of the year

Thin ice

Total white out

Turn up the heat

Walking in a winter wonderland

Warm up your winter

Welcome, winter!

When temps drop

Winter blues

Winter break

Winter chic

Winter crush

Winter formal

Winter games

Winter is coming

Winter warrior

Winter weather

Winter weather warning

Winter wishes

Winter wonderland

Winter's last breath

*For more inspiration, see **Christmas** on pg. 55 or **Weather** on pg. 174.

SPRING

A day in May

April showers

Bring on spring

First signs of spring

Fresh look at spring

Fresh start

Get some sun

Get your room in bloom

Go outside

Hello sunshine!

Hop into spring

In bloom

It's a spring thing

Rain, rain go away

Room in bloom

Scream spring

Shower power

Spring ahead

Spring air

Spring awakening

Spring break

Spring break in sight!

Spring break: It's on!

Spring celebrations

Spring cleaning

Spring dream

Spring dreaming

Spring energy

Spring essentials

Spring fever

Spring fling

Spring for florals & plaids

Spring forward

Spring greens

Spring has sprung!

Spring in sight

Spring in your step

Spring into action

Spring into…

Spring it on!

Spring pad

Spring rolls

Spring rules

Spring showers

Spring style

Spring up

Stand out for spring

Swing into spring

Think spring

Welcome spring

*For more inspiration, see
Florals on pg. 12 and
Weather on pg. 174.

SUMMER

Back to paradise

Bahama mama

Beach babe

Beach bash

Beach bods

Beach body

Beach bound

Beach cruiser

Beach honey

Beach toys

Beach within reach

Beauty & the beach

Brave the waves

Breaking waves

Bungalow

Cabana

Chill chica

Comfort zone

Create your own oasis

Dive in

Endless summer

Escape to paradise

Find a new paradise

Find your paradise

Floats your boat

Follow the sun

Fun in the sun

Get back to paradise

Get in your comfort zone…

Get ready to make waves!

Get some vitamin D

Get your beach on

Go coastal

Going coastal?

Hit the sand

Hot steals

Hot summer, cool deals

Hot tropic

In the swim of things

Island surf

Isle style

Jump

Just add water

Life's a beach!

Lifeguard on duty

Make a splash

Paradise calls

Reef retreat

Sand in sight?

Slice of paradise

So beachy

Sol sister

Splash down

Summer catch

Summer crush

Summer escape

Summer lovin'

Summer school

Sun in

Sunny day getaway

Sunny deals

Sunny delights

Sunny steals

Sunscreen weather

Take a dive

The coast is clear...

To the beach, please

Tropical oasis

Tropical retreat

Tropical spa

Under the sun

Warm-weather ready

Wave lengths...

*For more inspiration, see **Weather** on pg. 174 and **Swimsuits** on pg. 37.

FALL

A hunting we will go

All for fall

Apple picking

Autumn is calling

Boot season

Bountiful harvest

Bushels of fun

Celebrate the beauty
of the season

Changing leaves

Chase the chill

Crisp air

Crisp days of fall

Crisp weather

Fairs

Fall arrivals

Fall arrives

Fall calls

Fall colors

Fall faves

Fall favorites

Fall foliage

Fall forecast

Fall into…

Fall leaves

Fall palettes

Fall-ready…

Festival of fall color

Finally…fall!

First look at fall

Football season

Forever fall

Fresh color for fall

Fresh for fall

Gather all for fall

Get set for fall

Happy autumn

Happy fall

Harvest festivals

Harvest moon

Harvest of memories

Harvest season

Hello fall

Idyllic fall getaway

Indian summer

Jump into fall

Leaf-peeping

Leaves falling, autumn's calling

Let your leaves fall

October-fest

Oktoberfest

Open season on…

Pile on the…

Plan the perfect fall

Planning a memorable fall

Planning the perfect fall

Pumpkin patches

Pumpkin season

Pumpkin spice

Scarecrow

Scenic drives

Seasonal scenery

September mornings

Shades of fall

Splendor of fall

Sweater weather

The autumn leaves

The bounty of the season

The perfect fall getaway

Toasty

Traditions of the season

True colors

Turning over a new leaf

Vibrant

When fall calls

*For more inspiration, see **Weather** on pg. 174.

WEATHER

Baby it's cold outside

Beat the cold snap

Below zero

Break the ice

Brrrrr

Bundle up

Calm before the storm

Chance of rain

Chase the chill

Clear skies ahead

Cold front

Cold play

Cold wave

Come rain or come shine

Cooling down

Cuddle up

Dashing through the snow

Do a raindance

Eye of the hurricane

First alert

Freeze warning

Heavy weather

Hot enough to fry an egg

How's the weather?

Ice breakers

Ice over

Ice up

Icy-cool

In a fog

In the air

In the forecast

It's going to be a scorcher

Make it rain

Outfox Jack Frost

Partly cloudy

Rain check

Rain, rain go away

Rain ready

Raining cats and dogs

Shower power

Snow day

Stay cool out there

Stay warm out there

Storm out

Storms rolling in

Stormy weather

Take the heat

The big chill

The heat is on

Thin ice

Things are warming up

Triple digits

Turn up the heat

Warm up

Warm up your winter

Warming trends

Warming up

Weather permitting

Weather the storm

Weather watch

Wet weather

When it rains, it pours

When lightning strikes

Winter games

Winter weather warning

Winter wonderland

Wrap

You're getting warmer…

*For more inspiration, see **Seasons** on pg. 165.

SECTION 13:

SPORTS

BASEBALL

1, 2, 3 strikes, you're out

7th inning stretch

All about that base?

All-American

At bat

Ballgame basics

Baseball all day, every day

Baseball mad

Bases are loaded!

Bat a thousand

Bat stats

Batter up!

Batter's box

Big coverage of the big leagues

Big fly

Big league

Bleacher/stands in the ballpark

Bring the ballgame home

Buy me some peanuts and Cracker Jack

Catch the fever

Change-up

Cover all the bases

Cover your bases

Create a pitch-perfect…

Curve ball

Deuces are wild!

Do a double play

Don't drop the ball

Double base hit

Double clutch

Double header

Double steal

Double up

First pitch

Fly ball

For the ultimate fan:

Game-winning play

Get on deck

Go to bat for

Go pro

Grand slam

Great catch

Here's the pitch

Hey batter batter!

Hit a triple

Hit it out of the park

Hits, runs and steals

Home field advantage

Home fun

Home run

Home stretch

In the dugout

It's a whole new ballgame

Knock it out of the park

Knuckle ball

Live the dream

Major coverage of the Major League

Non-stop live action

On deck

On the mound

On the road

Perfect pitch

Pitch by pitch

Pitch perfect

Play ball!

Quick pitch

Raise your game

Root for the home team

Root, root, root for the home team

Slide into…

Spring training

Starting lineup

Steal a base

Step up to the plate!

Strike out

Strike zone

Strikeout

Take me out to the ball game

Take the field

Three-run hit

Two-base run

Two run hit

Umpire

Up at bat

Walk-off

What a catch!

What a play

What a steal!

Wild pitch

BASKETBALL

3-pointer…

A bank shot

Airball

Assist

Ball's in my/your court

Bank shot

Bench points

Big shot

Bounce off something

Bounce pass

Buzzer beater

Calling the shots

Carry the ball

Center

Center court

Chest pass

Dribble

Dunk

Fast break

Field goal

Foul shot

Free throw

Full-court heave

Full-court press

Get a jump on…

Goes for the shot

Halftime

He shoots, he scores

Hook shot

Hoop dreams…

Hot shot

In the paint

In the zone

It's a jump ball

Jump at the chance…

Jump shot

Keep one's eye on the ball

Layup

Long shot

Man-to-man coverage

March Madness

Not by a long shot

Nothing but net

Off the rim

On the ball

On the rebound

On the sidelines

Out of bounds

Pass fake

Power forward

Rebound

Score points with…

Set the pace

Shoot some hoops

Shooting range

Shot attempt

Shot caller

Shot clock

Sit on the sidelines

Skip pass

Slam dunk

Straight shooter

Swish!

Take a shot

Take charge

Take it to the hole

Take one's eye off the ball

That's the way the ball bounces

Three-point line

Three-point play

Tip-off

Traveling

Who calls the shots?

CHEERLEADING

[mascot] pride!

#1 fan

Are you game?

Attitude crew

Best. Mascot. Ever!

Best. Pre-game. Ever!

Campus crew

Campus pullover

Cheer life

Cheer squad

Crush those guys

Eat. Sleep. Cheer. Repeat.

Everything but the pom poms

Flip flip hooray

Fool 4 school

Game day spirit

Game for anything…

Gather your crew!

Get in the spirit

Get in the zone

Get ready 'cuz we're bringin' it!

Get ready to cheer your face off

Get ready to get rowdy!

Get ready to get your cheer on.

Get ready. Get excited. Get your cheer on!

Get rowdy!

Get the crowd going

Get your crew & get rowdy!

Go [team], go!

Go big or go home!

Go team

Go team, go!

Go, go, go!

Go! Fight! Win!

Got spirit?

Here to win!

I'm in the zone!

In with the crew

Instant pep rally

Let's get loud

Let's pre-game

Live. Love. Cheer.

Make a ruckus

Make some noise!

Makin' a ruckus

My school's better

Not for the faint of spirit!

Not your average pep rally

Playin' the field

Pre-game, post-game

Pre-party, post-game

Pump up the crowd

Rah-rah-ruckus!

Rally

Ready, set, cheer!

Ready, set, get loud!

Ready, set, get rowdy!

Represent!

Rootin' for the team

Rowdy

Ruckus maker

School pride

School spirit goes to the next level

Shake your spirit maker!

Show your spirit!

Show your stuff

Spirit check!

Spirit overdose! Can you handle it?

Spirit sprint

Spirit week

Start the ruckus

That's the spirit

The spirit rally to end all spirit rallies.

Time to play!

Varsity jersey

We're #1

We've got spirit!

FOOTBALL

#1 draft pick

#1 fan

#1 pick

All-pro

Almost better than halftime commercials

Almost better than the commercials

Are you ready for football?

Better than the halftime show

Big game gear

Big play

Big-name players

Blind-sided

Blitz

Blow the whistle

Can't wait for Friday night…

Change of possession

Clear eyes, full heart, can't lose

Draft

End zone

False start

First down

Friday night lights

Fumble

Game day

Game face

Game time

Game time decision

Game-day crowd…

Gear up

Get in the game

Get in the zone

Get your game on…

Go big at home

Go big or go home

Go fight win

Go long!

Good move!

Great pass

Gridiron

Hail Mary

Halftime show

Here's the kickoff

Home field

Home field advantage

Huddle up

In the huddle

In the zone

Interception

Key players

Linemen

Make the playoffs

Missing football already?

Move the goalposts

MVPs

Nice catch

No penalty

Offense

On the field

Pack the house

Pass play

Playbook

Player of the week

Punt

Punt returner

Rally

Receiver

Ruling on the field stands

Run interference

Running play

Rush the field...

Score!

Scramble

Scrimmage

Starting lineup

State bound

Super bowl

Take a timeout

Takin' the field

The big game

The blind side

The snap

Touchdown

Turnover

Up for grabs!

Varsity blues

Win over the crowd…

Winning field goal

Winning ticket

Winning touchdown

XX yards to go

GOLF

Above par

Below par

Birdie

Bogey

Bunkers

Caddyshack

Cart

Chipping greens

Club

Clubhouse

Doffing

Double bogey

Drive it home

Fire in the hole

Go long

Golf getaway

Grip it and rip it

Handicap

Hit the links

Hit your stride

Hitting the driver

Hole in one

Iron men

It's tee time

Lace up your spikes

Line up

Line up the perfect shot

Long drive

Love of the game

Nine-iron

Nineteenth hole

Off course

On the fairway

On the green

On the links

On the rough

Par for the course

Perfect round

Putting

Putting green

Score

Setup

Spruce up your game…

Stay the course

Step into spring

Step up your game

Swing

Take aim

Take it to the course

Tee it up

Tee off

Teeing ground

To a tee

Tread lightly…

Tree shot

Walk the course

Weekend warriors

What a shot

While the iron's hot

Who's your caddy?

Yards

Zinger

OLYMPICS

1st place	Gold medal
A lifetime of training	High jump
Action sports	High score
Adventure	Jump into the games!
Age-old tradition	Keep it real
All-extreme	Let the games begin
Big air	Medal count
Champion	Memorable moments
Closing ceremony	No limits
Double take	Olympics debut
Drop zone	Olympic flame
Faster, higher, stronger	Olympic games
First-place	Olympic legends
First-place finish	Olympic medal
Flip flip hooray	Olympic spirit
Game on!	Olympic-style...
Get a jump on...	On the edge
Get the gold	Opening ceremony
Go for gold	Perfect finish
Go for the gold	Perfect landing

Place 1st

Power play

Qualifies

Score big

Ski tour

Sound on/off

Special events

Team USA

The wire

Train hard

Wins gold

World-class...

World record

Worlds apart

SKIING / SNOWBOARDING

Adjust your altitude

All-mountain

Alley-oop

Alpine adventure

Apres ski

Atomic

Backcountry

Backflip

Backside

Barrel roll

Betty

Board length

Bonking the server

Carve out…

Cool 'n' out

First tracks

Follow my tracks

Forward lean

Freeride

Freeriding

Freestyle

Fresh powder

Fun on the slopes

Get strapped in

Give your … a 180

Going downhill

Grind

Half-pipe

Handrails

Heads up

Hit the slopes

Hit the snow

Launch

King of the hill

Method

Mountain makeover

Need a lift?

Peak…

Pipe

Powder field

Powder hound

Powder princess

Rewind

Rise and glide

Shredding

Sick tricks

Ski bums

Ski lift

Ski season

Sick…

Slope style

Slush

Snow bunny

Snow day

Snow ride

Stance

Straight air

Take it easy

Tracked out

Tricked out

White powder

Wipeout

SOCCER

Back of the net	High press
Best on the field	Hit me with your best shot
Chip shot	Hit the field
Corner kick	In the zone
Cover the field	It's a win-win
Danger zone	Kickin' it
Deliver the ball	Man to man
Drive	Midfield
Drop kick	Off sides
Empty net	Play the field
Fast break	Red card
Field day	Score
Full back	Scoring goals
Get a kick out of…	Shin guards
Get your kicks	Soccer star
Go for the goal	Squad goals
Good goalie	Take the field
Gooooooal!	Time to kick butt
Half-back	Winning goal
Header	World Cup

SURFING

100% summer

180/360

Bay watch

Beach bash

Beach bound

Beach break

Beach style

California dreaming

Coast into summer

Colossal

Curl crazy

Do the wave

Dreamin' of the perfect wave

Endless summer

Epic

Every day is a day at the beach

Genius

Get on board

Getting a jump on summer

Going coastal

Got the beach in your soul?

Hang ten

Heavy waves

Here comes the sun

High jump

I dare you…

In the zone

Isle style

It's your wave!

Kids of summer

Legendary

Let's ride

Looking for the perfect wave

Make waves

Make your move

New waves

Nothing says summer like surf

On the scene

Our place in the sun

Pipeline

Planning the escape

Pool cues

Pool party

School's out, surf's up!

Shades of summer

Shady business

Shore thing

Stoked

Summer catch

Summer fever

Summer of surf

Summerland

Sun-day style

Sunny delight

Surf & turf

Surf city!

Surf finds

Surf in sight

Surf style

Surf to your turf

Surf-cool

Surfari

Surfside

Surfsite

Take five

Wavelengths

Wetsuit

Wipe-out

MISCELLANEOUS SPORTS SAYINGS

A fighting chance

A game changer

A losing game

Across the board

Ahead of the game

At this stage in the game

Be a bad sport

Be a good sport

Bring your A game

Call the shots

Clear a hurdle

Come out swinging

Dive in headfirst

Down for the count

Down to the wire

Drop the ball

Elevate your game

First out of the gate

First-string

For the win

Full-court press

Get a head start

Get a second wind

Get in the game

Get off to a flying start

Get the ball rolling

Get your game on!

Go to bat for

Go to the mat for

Go, fight, win!

Hard to call

Have the inside track

Have the upper hand

Hit below the belt

Hot shot

In full swing

In the home stretch

It's a whole new ballgame

It's all fun and games until…

It's game over

It's gametime

Jump the gun

Jump through hoops

Learn the ropes

Long shot

Make the cut

Meet one's match

Miss the cut

Neck and neck

New to the game

No holds barred

No sweat

Odds are against

Off and running

Off your game

On deck

Out of left field

Out of someone's league

Par for the course

Pass the torch

Play hardball

Play-by-play

Play by the rules

Playing the long game

Put on your gameface

Race against the clock

Raise your game

Rally around…

Roll with the punches

Rookie move

Safe bet

Score points with…

Set the pace

Shut 'em down

Shutout

Sink or swim

Skin in the game

Sore loser

Spectator sport

Sports Central

Sports Fan Central

Sports Fan Destination

Sports fan must-haves

Sports Headquarters

Sports lineup

Sports Stop

Star power

Start the ball rolling

Step up your game

Tackle a problem

Take aim at…

Take the bull by the horns

Team player

That's the name of the game

The ball's in my/your court

The front runner

The game is up

The rules of the game

Throw in the towel

Toe the line

Warm the bench

We are the champions

We've got your game

What's the score?

What's your game plan?

What's your game?

What's your sport?

Who's your team?

Wild card

SECTION 14:

TRAVEL

CAMPING

A call of nature	Gather 'round the fire
Around the fire	Gear to go
Back to nature	Get back to nature
Back to the basics	Get going
Backcountry basics	Get set
Backcountry bound	Get your gear
Blaze a new trail	Go beyond
Blaze a trail	Happy camper
Bon voyage	Hike in
Bonfire nights	Hit the road
Break camp	Hot on the trail
Build a campfire	It's a summer thing
Cabin fever	It's no picnic
Call of the wild	Keep calm and camp on
Calling all campers	Let's go camping
Camp out	Make tracks
Camp-cooking	Middle of nowhere
Campfire classics	Mother Nature
Camping champ	On the trail
Escape	Out of the woods

Pack your bags

Peace and quiet

Pitch a tent

Pitch camp

Pull up stakes

Roughing it

S'more fun

Set up camp

Sleeping under the stars

Stake a claim

Summer adventures

Summer camp

Summer fling

Take a hike

Take it outside

Tent's up

The great unknown

The howl of wolves

The nature of adventure

The outback

The outside world

Trail head

Trail's end

Weekend forecast

Woodland creatures

Your neck of the woods

DISTANCE

Around the block	Local discoveries
Around the corner	Local happenings
At the … in your area	Miles away
At the … near you	Miles to go
At your local…	Near the mark
Close to home	Near you
Close to you	Near you now
Close by	Near you soon
Country mile	Nearby
Drop in…	New and near you
In your area	New and nearby
Near you	Next door
Far and wide	Not anywhere near
Far from it	Not far out
Far out	Nowhere near
From your local …	On your map
In your area	On your radar
In your neck of the woods	Right next door
In your vicinity	So close
Just a drive away	So close and yet so far

So near and yet so far

Steps away

Stop by…

Swing by…

The far side

Within reach

Within your area

Within your reach

Your neighborhood…

FLIGHT

Above the clouds

Air pocket

Air traffic control

Airborne

Airport lounge

Aisle seats

All systems go!

Around the world

At the gate

At the terminal

Attendants

Baggage claim

Basic training

Boarding pass

Book your travel

Cabin crew

Check the status

Check your bags

Check-in

Co-pilot

Command center

Control room

Control tower

Cool your jets

Core mission

Cross check

Cruising altitude

Deplane

Destination

Direct flight

Early arrival

Early departure

Elevate

ETA

Exit row

Fasten your seatbelts

Final approach

First class

Flight

Flight deck

Flight delays

Flight of your life

Flight plan

Fly by the seat of your pants

Fly coach

Fly the friendly skies

Flying high

Free flight

From takeoff to landing

Full upright and locked position

Getaway

Global

Grounded

Holding pattern

In-flight entertainment

Itinerary

Keep the aisles clear

Late departure

Launch

Layover

Leavin' on a jetplane

Loop the loop

Lost and found

Main cabin

Mission

Mission control

Mission ready

Nail the landing

Nonstop

Now boarding

On autopilot

On board

On-time

One way

Pilot

Plane

Please remain seated

Preboard

Prepare for takeoff

Return flight

Roundtrip

Security line

Smooth landing

Soar

Steer the plane

Steer through

Take a nosedive

Takeoff

Top flight

Track flights

Travel guide

Travel time

Turbulence

Wheels down

Wheels up

Window seats

Wings

Your mission is simple

GEAR (BAGS AND LUGGAGE)

00" inches of storage

A soft spot for laptops

Bag claim

Bag it up

Bag it!

Bag, you're it.

Baggage check

Baggage claim

Bags are packed

Carry-on

Claim your bag

Details are everything

Divide and hide

Fold it up & go

Fully equipped

Get a handle on things

Get carried away

Grab it, stuff it, love it!

Handle with flair

Have wheels, will travel.

Hot wheels, happy feet.

It's in the bag!

Jam-packed!

Knapsacks

Let's sort things out

Load it up!

Master multitasker

Multitasking master

New and tote-worthy

P is for pocket

Pack attack

Pack it up, pack it in

Pack your bags

Pack your bags and leave tonight

Packs stacked with features

Put more stuff in here

Roll if you want to

Roll with it

Roomy enough for your biggest...

Sort it out

Store more, spend less

Superfly (zippers)

Take a load off

The essentials for your essentials

Travel light

Totally tote-worthy

We got your back

We got your pack

HOTEL / ACCOMMODATIONS

All the amenities

Bellboy/bellhop

Check in (v.)/check-in (adj)

Check out (v.)/checkout (adj)

Complimentary…

Concierge service

Connecting rooms

Continental breakfast

Customer satisfaction

Customer service

Do not disturb

Double occupancy

Early check-in

Early departure

Enjoy your stay

First-class

Five-star

Friendly greeting

Friendly service

Gracious host

Greet guests

Hit snooze

Hospitality

Housekeeping

How was your stay?

It's my pleasure

Late checkout

Nightcap

No vacancy

Ocean view room

On the grounds

On-site

Raid the minibar

Reception

Room key

Room number

Room service

Room with a view

Shuttle service

Single occupancy

Sleep in

Staff

Suite retreat

Tip included

Turndown service

Upon check-in

Valet parking

Wake-up call

Warm welcome

Welcome bag

X-Star Rating

TRAVEL

A mile a minute

Adventure

Along for the ride

At a crossroads

Au revoir!

Backseat driver

Beyond the…

Bon voyage

Bound for…

Coast into…

Cross country

Destination inspiration

Don't rock the boat

Escape

Final destination

Fly high

Fork in the road

Gear to go!

Gear up

Get going!

Get packed

Get set

Get your gear

Getaway

Go beyond

Go off the rails

Go the extra mile

Have…, will travel

Here comes the sun…

Hit a roadblock

Hit the road

In high gear

In the driver's seat

In the home stretch

In the same boat

Jet set

Just traveling through

Make tracks

Middle of nowhere

Middle of the road

Off the beaten path

On the right track

Pack your bags

Path less taken

Path less traveled

Ready, set, go

Ready, set, jet

Road rage

Roadtrips

Roll with the punches

Running on fumes

Shift gears

Ship has sailed

Sightseeing

Step out

Style-packed bags

Take a hike

Take a trip

Take five…

Take it outside…

Turn the corner

Wild ride

Your own backyard

*For more inspiration, see **Flight** on pg. 204.

ADDITIONAL RESOURCES

• **Words that Sell, Revised and Expanded Edition: The Thesaurus to Help You Promote Your Products, Services, and Ideas** (2006) by Richard Bayan

• **Phrases that Sell, The Ultimate Phrase Finder to Help You Promote Your Products, Services, and Ideas** (1998) by Edward Werz and Sally Germain

• **The Elements of Style** (2000) by William Strunk Jr. and E.B. White

• **Ogilvy on Advertising** (1985) by David Ogilvy

• **Net Words: Creating High-Impact Online Copy** (2002) by Nick Usborne

• **Powerlines: Words that Sell Brands, Grip Fans and Sometimes Change History** (2008) by Steve Cone

ABOUT THE AUTHOR

LIZETTE RESENDEZ has spent the last 15 years as a copywriter, content strategist and digital storyteller, creating marketing concepts for a variety of Fortune 500 clients including Oracle, Comcast, The Ritz-Carlton, LEGO, Harley-Davidson, Pottery Barn, ANN Taylor and Victoria's Secret.

She graduated from Texas A&M University with a bachelor's degree in journalism. She currently lives in Austin, TX with her husband and son.

Printed in Great Britain
by Amazon